WILLIAM WINSTANLEY

*Engraving of William Winstanley
published by William Richardson,
a famous London print-seller,
in 1677.
By courtesy of Mr Christopher Rowe*

WILLIAM WINSTANLEY

THE MAN
WHO SAVED
CHRISTMAS

by
Alison Barnes

POPPYLAND
PUBLISHING

Published by Poppyland Publishing, Cromer, NR27 9AN

Designed and typeset in 12 on 16pt Golden Cockerel by Watermark, Cromer, NR27 9HL

Printed by Barnwell's, Aylsham

ACKNOWLEDGEMENTS

Many people have helped with the research for this book and the author is extremely grateful to them all, but would like to thank in particular the Rev. Frank Best, Mr Martyn Everett, Mr Len Pole, Mr Christopher Rowe, Mr Norman Stanley, Mr Malcolm White, the staff of the Bodleian Library, the staff of the British Library, the staff of Chelmsford Library, the staff of the Guildhall Library, London, the staff of the Essex Record Office and the staff of Saffron Walden Museum.

*To the people of
Quendon,
Saffron Walden
& Littlebury*

PREFACE

WILLIAM WINSTANLEY, poet, journalist, historian and uncle to Henry Winstanley, builder of the first Eddystone lighthouse, was one of the most popular writers in England in the latter part of the seventeenth century, his works being admired by such notables as King Charles II, the first Duke of Beaufort and John Evelyn, as well as by the majority of the reading public. Many of his books continued to be reprinted right down to Victorian times, and they are still of use to modern historians for the light they shed on seventeenth-century social life.

Winstanley's chief claim to fame today, however, is that he saved our traditional English Christmas customs for us. Throughout the Interregnum the Puritans under Oliver Cromwell had banned all Christmas festivities, so that by the time Charles II was restored to the throne in 1660 these celebrations had become almost extinct in England, and had it not been for the tireless press campaign that William mounted to revive and promote them, it seems likely that many of our favourite Christmas traditions would have died out by the end of the seventeenth century, and we would not now be enjoying our Christmas turkeys, mince pies, decorations, games and carols.

William Winstanley himself celebrated Christmas with a zest and cordiality that have probably never been surpassed in England. And the main purpose of this book is to describe the numerous fascinating rituals and festivities that took place annually in Winstanley's large Essex farmhouse called Berries from 1670 to 1698. Taken together, these varied observances afford us an unparalleled insight into what a seventeenth-century English country Christmas was really like.

In order to explain why William Winstanley was so passionately fond of Christmas, and how he came to champion the festival, it has been necessary to devote the first chapter of the book to tracing his family background and personal history. This information has been obtained from the vast collection of wills, deeds, leases, account books, court rolls and private papers pertaining to the Essex branch of the Winstanley family that are lodged at the Bodleian Library, the British Library, the Essex Record Office, Saffron Walden Museum and Saffron Walden Town Library, as well as from Winstanley's own multitudinous writings.

The documentary material has hitherto remained virtually unknown. But it repays study, for it not only reveals many intriguing new facts about both William Winstanley and his famous nephew Henry, but also shows that the Essex Winstanleys as a whole were one of the most delightful families who have ever lived in the county.

CONTENTS

Engraving of Saffron Walden High Street
from Thomas Wright's History of Essex, *1832.*
It looked almost identical in the late seventeenth century.

INTRODUCTION

IN THE SPRING of 1621, William Winstanley's father, Henry Winstanley, a prosperous London lawyer, suddenly decided that he had had enough of the crowded City and would like to turn yeoman and live in the country. His cousin and close friend James Wilford owned Quendon Hall, a fine Tudor manor house in Quendon, a hamlet five miles south of Saffron Walden, Essex, where he had spent many pleasant holidays. So he determined to settle in that locality.

The Winstanley clan originated from the village of Winstanley, five miles south-west of Wigan, Lancashire, where they were established at Winstanley Hall, a large moated manor, by 1150. In the early sixteenth century, however, the Winstanleys fell on hard times, and younger branches of the family began to migrate to other parts of England; Henry's kin settling at Hartridge, Kent, where they intermarried with the Wilfords.

By 1580 both families had left Kent for London, and here they flourished exceedingly. In about 1600 James Wilford met Anne Newman, daughter and sole heiress of Thomas Newman of Quendon Hall, when she was on a visit to the Metropolis, married her, and as her father had died in 1586, became the new Lord of the Manor.

Whilst looking for a suitable farm round Quendon, Henry Winstanley stayed with James, his wife and their six children, and renewed his acquaintance with all the principal landowners of north-west Essex, including Theophilus Howard, second Earl of Suffolk at Audley End, Timothy Middleton of Stansted Hall and the wealthy farmer-cum-merchant Leader family of Saffron Walden.

By the early summer of 1621, Mr Winstanley had fallen in love with pretty, vivacious Elizabeth Leader, the sixteen-year-old daughter of Samuel Leader, a rich Walden merchant. And in September he married the girl and went to live with her in a beautiful Tudor farmhouse called Berries that he had bought in Quendon.

The house was surrounded by a two-acre garden, and as well as cultivating this plot, Henry Winstanley farmed a further hundred acres of land at Quendon that he leased from the Wilfords. He also bought various pieces of freehold land and several houses at Rickling, Littlebury, Audley End, Saffron Walden and Newport. Possessing an innate feeling for the soil, Henry thrived as a farmer, and he occasionally made a little extra money by acting as an attorney for the Wilfords and other friends and neighbours. Very soon he had become a much respected figure in the district, whose advice was sought on a whole range of legal and agricultural matters, and whose friendship was greatly valued.

Elizabeth, too, prospered at Quendon. She diligently studied

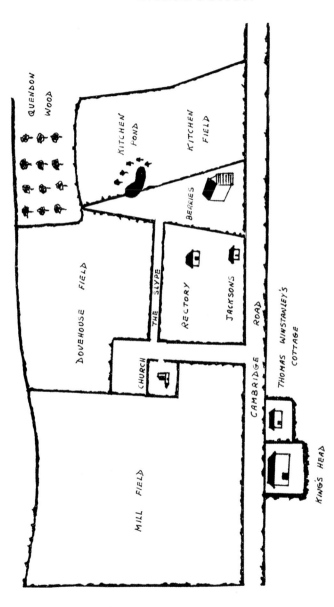

Sketch map of Quendon based on the Quendon Hall estate map of 1645.

both cookery and herbal medicine, and quickly gained a reputation for being a very good cook and a skilled physician who could cure most ailments with her herbal remedies. Between 1622 and 1640 she also produced eight children; four boys, Thomas, Henry, William and James and four girls, Elizabeth, Anne, Mary and Susan, of whom William, born in 1628, was the third son.

In many ways the Quendon Winstanleys were a typical yeoman family; hearty, hospitable, very fond of one another and intensely loyal to Church and King. They were rather more cultured than most farming folk of that day, however. For Henry the elder had a wide knowledge of history, the classics and English literature, and on winter evenings would either tell thrilling stories about the heroes of old, or read aloud from his favourite books such as Chaucer's *Canterbury Tales* or Spenser's *Faerie Queene*. He was extremely interested in folk customs, too, and saw to it that his family celebrated traditional English festivals like Valentine's Day, May Day and Guy Fawkes' Night with all due ceremony.

But the feast that the Winstanleys liked best was undoubtedly Christmas. Being devout Anglicans Henry and Elizabeth considered that the birth of Christ was 'the best Newes that was ever brought to us since the World began'. They believed that this supremely joyful event should be commemorated not only by prayer, church services and the singing of carols, but also by those secular observances that engendered good fellowship and innocent mirth. Throughout the Twelve Days of Christmas, therefore, the family kept open house at Berries, danced, played games, told ghost and fairy tales round the hearth and invited all their relatives, friends and needy neighbours to partake of the delicious Christmas fare provided by Elizabeth.

These idyllic Christmas holidays of his boyhood aroused in William Winstanley a passionate love for this great festival and from an early age inspired him to find out all he could about Yuletide customs, legends and traditions. Like his father, William delighted in folklore, history and English literature. He was equally fascinated by his mother's herbal remedies, and often helped her prepare her concoctions in the still-room at Berries. He loved music, art and architecture, too, and excelled at all sports, especially football. By nature he was very kind-hearted, and possessed a lively sense of humour and a fertile imagination. He also had a charismatic charm of manner which made him beloved by everyone who knew him.

William's exceptional intelligence attracted the attention of Theophilus Howard and Timothy Middleton, who gave him the run of their libraries and encouraged him in his studies. What formal education the boy received is not known. He does not appear to have attended the famous Grammar Schools at Saffron Walden or Newport, and was probably taught the classics, and other subjects such as history, geography and mathematics either by his father or by the learned rector of Quendon, Job Hawker, whose rectory adjoined Berries.

At the age of fourteen William Winstanley was apprenticed to his uncle, William Leader, a wealthy Saffron Walden mercer-cum-linen-draper. He knew by this time that he wished to be a writer, an ambition that his father may well have helped to foster. But he wanted the boy to have a good trade to fall back on in case of need, and insisted that he complete his apprenticeship. William Leader so admired his nephew's poems and tales, however, that he accorded him much leisure in which to practise writing. During the last two years of William's apprenticeship, from 1647 to 1649, he even allowed him to make frequent trips to London to begin research for his masterpiece *England's Worthies*, which was finally published in 1659 to universal acclaim.

Whilst in the Metropolis, William Winstanley met and was befriended by many scholarly and influential men including the historian Thomas Fuller, John Taylor the 'Water Poet' and Charles Dormer, Earl of Caernarfon. His chief patron, however, was Henry Somerset, Lord Herbert, the future first Duke of Beaufort, who was impressed by his wit and sagacity and did everything he could to advance him in his career.

All these men were staunch Royalists, as was William himself, and as well as talking about history, art and literature they often discussed the various atrocities perpetrated by the Puritan Parliament under Oliver Cromwell. The beheading of Charles I at Whitehall on 30th January 1649 was of course the worst of these iniquities. But to William the determined efforts Parliament was making to exterminate his favourite festival – Christmas – seemed almost as bad.

The Puritans hated Christmas because of its 'Popish' and 'Heathenish' antecedents, and its associations with drinking, dancing and acting, all of which pastimes were anathema to them. And between 1644 and 1647 Parliament introduced a series of measures

Portrait of Henry Somerset, first Duke of Beaufort,
attributed to the studio of Sir Peter Lely.
From the collection of the Duke of Beaufort.

aimed at curbing the feast. This legislation had little effect on the population at large, who for several years flatly refused to give up their Christmas junketings. Finally, however, on 24th December, 1652, Parliament issued a Proclamation stating that from thenceforth it would be strictly illegal to observe 'the Five and twentieth day of December, commonly called Christmas-Day' in any way whatsoever, or to use 'any Solemnity in Churches upon that Day in respect thereof'. Markets were ordered to be kept, shops to remain open, and all persons to go about their normal business on Christmas Day. And the country's sheriffs and JPs were instructed to enforce this new ruling with the utmost rigour of the law.

William Winstanley and his family took no notice of this edict, and throughout the Interregnum bravely continued to celebrate Christmas with all their wonted jollity. They were unable to attend Divine Service at Christmas as the doors of Quendon Church were locked by the Puritans on that day from 1652 to 1659. But to compensate they held a prayer and carol service of their own devising in the hall at Berries.

By 1652 William had completed his apprenticeship to William Leader and was living with his first wife Martha and their baby son Will in a house in Creepmouse Alley, just off the Market Square in Saffron Walden. His father had died in 1646, leaving Elizabeth to run the farm alone, which she did very competently. She liked to have all her children and grandchildren about her at Christmas, however. So William and his brothers and sisters accompanied by their spouses and offspring always spent the Yuletide holidays in Quendon.

Like the Winstanleys, many other families in England ignored Parliament's prohibition of Christmas and commemorated the feast in the time-honoured ways. But either through fear or inclination a large number of people did not celebrate the festival at all during the Commonwealth. This weakened the position of Christmas in the country as a whole, so that even after the Restoration in 1660, when everyone was free to keep the holiday as they wished, it failed to regain the universal popularity that it had enjoyed in the 1630s, and was in fact in danger of dying out altogether.

Sketch based on a woodcut of 1652, depicting Old Christmas, the personification of the Yuletide festivities that were banned by the Puritans in that year.

William Winstanley viewed this decline of Christmas with deep dismay. As devoutly religious as his parents, he believed that it was the duty of all Christians to celebrate the birth of their Saviour with joyous festivity and open-handed generosity towards friends, relations and more especially the poor. Ever a kind benefactor to the poor of north-west Essex, he recognised

19

how immensely important to the destitute was the feasting and entertainment provided for them yearly at Christmas by the rich. For it gave them something to look forward to in the cold, dark days of November and December, and supplied a stock of heartening memories to tide them over till spring.

William thought that the numerous pleasant old customs that had been associated with Christmas from time immemorial should also be kept up as they promoted conviviality and added zest to the proceedings. He determined, therefore, to do everything he could to revive interest in Christmas and preserve the festival for posterity. And from 1662 until his death in 1698 he conducted a vigorous campaign to this end, both through personal contacts and through the press.

By the early 1660s William Winstanley had published a very popular book of poems, *The Muses Cabinet*, two of his most famous biographical works, *England's Worthies* and *The Loyall Martyrology*, and a compendium of useful information, *The Pathway to Knowledge*, and had become one of the most sought after literary figures in England. This fame led to his meeting a vast number of people in many different parts of the country and in all walks of life. And making full use of his persuasive charm he cajoled these myriad acquaintances into observing the complete religious and secular rites of the traditional English Christmas. His many powerful patrons such as Lord Herbert and the Earl of Suffolk zealously assisted him in this cause, not only keeping Christmas in lavish style themselves but urging their relations, friends and tenants to do likewise.

To encourage the general public to celebrate Christmas in a fitting manner, Winstanley annually produced a stream of books, pamphlets, articles and poems praising the festival and extolling its joys, some of these works being published under his own name, others under the pseudonym Poor Robin that he adopted in 1661. How this *nom de plume* originated is not known for certain, but in his youth William did a lot of research on the poor, ragged, merry country fairy Robin Goodfellow, who was thought to perform domestic tasks for worthy farmers and keep a benign eye on their cattle and crops. It is probable that helping on his parents' farm himself and possessing as merry a heart as Robin, the boy identified somewhat with this puckish sprite and adopted his name.

In Victorian times controversy raged in the literary world as to whether the appellation Poor Robin rightfully belonged to William Winstanley, his nephew Robert Winstanley or the poet Robert Herrick, but there is in fact no doubt that Poor Robin was William's pseudonym. In his *Poor Robin's Almanack* for 1671 the author tells us that his true name is 'William Windstanley', and the clerk who recorded Winstanley's burial in 1698 in the Quendon Parish Registers included the words 'Cognomine Poor Robin' in his entry.

The series of *Poor Robin's Almanacks* that Winstanley published yearly from 1661 onwards were not the usual astrological almanacs, but rather witty burlesques filled with poems, jokes, riddles, culinary tips, seasonal lore, snippets of Essex and London gossip and many details about William Winstanley's own family. This mixture of zany humour and practical information proved irresistible to the public, and from their first appearance these almanacs were runaway bestsellers, eagerly snapped up every winter by the nobility and gentry as well as the literate working classes. So exceedingly popular had they become, indeed, by the time of Winstanley's death that they were continued by members of the Stationers' Company right down to 1827.

King Charles II was very fond of William Winstanley's almanacs and kept them all in his library at Whitehall. William had been introduced to the King soon after the Restoration by James Howard, third Earl of Suffolk, the Winstanleys' close friend, and the monarch had been so favourably impressed by him that throughout the 1660s he invited the writer to attend various Court functions, at which gatherings the pair laughed and joked together and played games of cards and crambo.

In the 1670s Winstanley became somewhat disillusioned by the fickle, pleasure-loving King. He remained faithful to Charles II until the end, however, and five years after his death described him in his *Poor Robin's Almanack* for 1690 as 'Just of his Word and Kind of Nature, the Magazin of Clemency, Fountain of Liberality and Pattern Patron of good Arts'.

Written in similar vein to Winstanley's almanacs and almost as popular was the weekly newspaper *Poor Robin's Intelligence* that he produced from 1676 until his death. As both the almanacs and the newspaper enjoyed an exceptionally wide readership, he considered that they were the ideal publications in which to set forth his views on Christmas and its festivities, and most of his Christmas writings are to be found in their pages. The remainder appear in the *Protestant Almanack* and the *Quakers' Almanack* that he brought out on an occasional basis, and in his books *Poor Robins Hue and Cry after Good Housekeeping, The Pathway to Knowledge* and the *New Help to Discourse,* these last two being reprinted almost every Christmas.

Throughout the thirty-eight years that William Winstanley wrote about Christmas, his attitude towards the festival and notions of how it ought to be kept remained virtually unchanged. First and foremost he believed that the 'Feast of the Nativity' should be a time of 'much mirth and mickle glee', when everyone rejoiced at the birth of the Divine Child and, for his sake, 'gave liberally to the poor' and 'provided good cheer for all friends and neighbours'. In honour of the season houses should, he thought, be decked out from top to bottom with 'Holly and Ivy, Bays, Laurel and Rosemary'. There should be 'Roaring log fires' in every room, and an especially 'jolly blaze' in the hall.

For the entertainment of guests 'good, nappy ale' should be always on tap throughout the Twelve Days of Christmas, and 'Bowls of Lambswool' in brisk circulation. The tables of the rich should groan under the weight of 'Chines of Beef, turkeys, geese, ducks and capons' and on the sideboard there ought to repose a plentiful supply of 'Minc'd Pies, Plumb-puddings and Frumenty'. All this traditional Christmas fare had been severely frowned upon by the Puritans, who condemned those who partook of it as 'Papists and Idolaters'. But after the return of 'Good King Charles' it was quite safe to enjoy such food again, and Winstanley exhorted his readers to offer their guests as many traditional dishes as possible so as to bring them back into favour.

He also exhorted them to play all the old Christmas games such as 'Hoodman Blind, Hot Cockles, Shoe the Wild Mare, Hunt the Slipper, Hide-and-Seek and Stool-Ball'. Other seasonal pastimes that he recommended were chess, backgammon, card and dice games, carol singing and story-telling. But the greatest fun of all, he considered, was to hold a dance after supper on Christmas Day, New Year's Eve or Twelfth Night and have 'the whole Company, young and old, footing it lustily to the merry sound of the pipe and fiddle'.

As well as annually describing a variety of Christmas customs that he hoped all his readers would adopt, Winstanley constantly urged the better off amongst them to emulate those archetypal 'boon brave Squires' of the 'Golden Age', who always returned to their country seats at Christmas, kept open house for all and sundry, lavished charity on the poor and were punctilious in observing their religious duties.

So persistently did he write about Christmas, and with such infectious enthusiasm, that by the late 1680s his views as to how the festival ought ideally to be celebrated had become accepted as the norm, and the traditional English Christmas that he advocated was back in fashion again.

The feast retained its popularity for twenty or so years after William Winstanley's death. Throughout that period his ideas about Christmas remained in the National consciousness and were further disseminated by writers such as Jonathan Swift, Alexander Pope and Joseph Addison, all three of whom much admired his Yuletide writings and often quoted from them. Addison, indeed, who as a young man in London had been a protégé of Winstanley's, based his kind, hospitable country squire Sir Roger de Coverley on his mentor's conception of the perfect squires of antiquity. His account of Sir Roger's Christmas festivities in Worcestershire appears to be an amalgam of several of Winstanley's Christmas articles in the *Poor Robin's Almanacks*.

By 1750 the traditional English Christmas had fallen into a second deep decline. By 1800 it was virtually extinct. In 1820, however, the festival suddenly took on a new lease of life – mainly due to the influence of William Winstanley.

It all began in 1819, when, in the process of doing research on English folklore at the British Museum, the genial American antiquarian Washington Irving stumbled across Winstanley's Christmas writings and was instantly captivated by their evocative descriptions of all those old 'holiday customs and rural games' that he most delighted in reading about. Irving found the numerous Christmas rites and rituals that Winstanley depicts so inspiring, in fact, that he decided to create an imaginary English Christmas of his own into which they could be incorporated.

The five Christmas essays detailing the Yuletide celebrations at Bracebridge Hall that grew out of this resolve not only faithfully reflect all William Winstanley's views about the festival and how it should be kept by wealthy squires, but also mention all his favourite Christmas dishes, games and pastimes and include several of his Christmas songs and poems. More importantly, however, these essays are permeated through and through with the same radiant joy, the same heart-warming benevolence that are the hallmarks of Winstanley's Christmas writings.

It was this tone of exuberant joviality that made Washington Irving's Christmas essays so immensely successful when they first appeared in England in 1820, published in his *Sketch Book*. Their popularity resulted in an immediate nation-wide revival of interest in the old traditional English Christmas customs; a revival which was strengthened and consolidated in the 1830s and 1840s by Charles Dickens' *Pickwick Papers* and *A Christmas Carol*.

Dickens' brilliant descriptions of the merry Christmas that Mr Pickwick and his friends enjoyed at Dingley Dell, and of the more modest but equally convivial Christmas festivities indulged in by the families of Bob Cratchit and Scrooge's nephew, finally transformed our English Christmas from the indifferently kept festival of 1800 into the phenomenally popular feast beloved by adults and children alike that it had become by 1850, and by and large still remains today. This crucial turning-point in the history of Christmas once again owed much to the influence of William Winstanley. Just as Winstanley's Christmas writings had inspired those of Washington Irving, so Irving's Yuletide essays inspired Dickens.

Washington Irving was the living author whom Dickens most admired. He kept all Irving's books on his library shelves, and is reputed to have had 'an intimate knowledge of them'. The Christmas essays in the *Sketch Book* were what impressed him most, however, and he readily admitted that the Dingley Dell chapters in *Pickwick* and several parts of the *Christmas Carol* owed a great deal to them.

A roaring log fire as depicted by Randolph Caldicott in Old Christmas, *the collection of five Christmas essays from Washington Irving's* Sketch Book, *published by the artist in 1875.*

Because we are still so familiar today with the Christmas writings of Washington Irving and Charles Dickens, we have come to believe that these two men between them formed the basic pattern of our traditional English Christmas. In reality, however, all the essential elements that constitute our vision of the 'ideal' English Christmas – log fires, evergreen decorations, special Yuletide fare, traditional games and carols, mirth, jollity and goodwill – do not stem from the literary tradition of Irving and Dickens but from that of William Winstanley, who after the Restoration selected the old Christmas observances that he thought most suitable to the season and through ceaseless cajolery and exhortation eventually succeeded in reviving public interest in them. These customs were so little kept up by 1660 that had he not made vigorous efforts to resuscitate them they would doubtless have greatly declined by the end of the seventeenth century and perhaps been lost to us.

Winstanley not only urged all his readers and acquaintances to commemorate Christmas in hearty style, but practised what he preached by celebrating the whole Twelve Days of the festival with enormous gusto himself. Ever since his boyhood, Christmas at Berries had always been observed with joyous revelry, but when he inherited the farm after his mother's death in 1670, he introduced a series of delightful innovations to the festivities which lent them a quite new enchantment. The graphic descriptions of his Christmas revels that Winstanley gives us in his almanacs, newspapers and books, together with the numerous details about the author and his family that can be gleaned from documents, provide a very clear picture of what these festivities were like and bring them vividly to life.

The fictional Christmas celebrations that were held at Washington Irving's Bracebridge Hall and Charles Dickens' Manor Farm, Dingley Dell, are regarded nowadays as the epitome of Yuletide jollification. But the real Christmas festivities that took place at Berries every year from 1670 to 1698 far surpassed these celebrations in. 'mirth and wassail', and were probably, indeed, the merriest Christmas junketings that have ever been enjoyed in England in any age.

Yuletide fare;
one of Randolph Caldicott's illustrations from Old Christmas.

PREPARATIONS

BERRIES was an ideal house in which to hold Christmas revelry. It was large enough to accommodate numerous guests, yet sufficiently compact always to feel snug and warm. Indoors the farm was comfortably and tastefully furnished throughout; externally the mellow red tiles on the roof and protective white weather-boarding that covered the sides gave the building a friendly, welcoming air that accorded well with the festive season. The extensive garden that surrounded the house provided ample space for outdoor gambols, and contained an orchard at one end where the apple trees were wassailed on Twelfth Night, and a big pond at the other, which was transformed into a perfect skating rink in frosty weather. Immediately behind the garden lay ancient, mysterious Quendon Wood, from which the Winstanleys obtained their Christmas greenery and their supply of logs.

Unfortunately Berries was pulled down some time between 1806 and 1838, and the only pictorial representations of the farm now extant are to be found on the Quendon Hall estate maps of 1645 and 1702. The first of these maps depicts the house as a long, tall, south-facing dwelling with tiled roof and weather-boarded sides. The second merely shows it as a stylised square box, but both indicate that Berries stood well back from the main road, more or less in the position now occupied by the modern rectory at Quendon.

Built in about 1550, Berries appears to have been a typical Essex timber-framed farmhouse of the period. From Winstanley wills and other documents we learn that on the ground floor there was a spacious hall with an inglenook fireplace, a parlour, a kitchen, a pantry, a still-room and a dairy. Upstairs a series of small bedrooms led off either side from the master bedroom in the middle. Somewhere on the second floor there was also a large 'soller' (solar), in which William Winstanley tells us that he stored bunches of dried herbs, jars of honey, sacks of nuts and row upon row of the pippins, codlings and warden pears that he grew in the orchard.

As was customary in seventeenth-century Essex farmhouses, most of the rooms at Berries would probably have had whitewashed walls with exposed beams, although the parlour here was wainscoted. The oak floors of the parlour and hall were covered with 'Turkey carpets'. But the less important downstairs rooms and most of the bedrooms are likely to have had thick rush matting on the floor as was then the norm.

We are told that the hall contained a long dining table, a sideboard, a settle and a variety of chairs, stools and benches. In the parlour there was a smaller table for informal family meals, some chairs and stools, the best spare bed and a dresser on which were ranged the choicest pieces from the large collection of pewter that William Winstanley had inherited from his mother, whose pride and joy it had been.

In the latter part of the seventeenth century such family pewter collections usually comprised a few chargers and dishes, several flagons, tankards, cups, salts, porringers and candlesticks and a great many mugs, bowls, plates and spoons. All these items might be decorated with beaded borders, mouldings, flutings or engravings, which added to their beauty. But even when quite plain, seventeenth-century pewter was always visually pleasing because of its harmonious shapes.

By 1670 William himself had built up a small collection of silver – some candlesticks, two or three salts, a wassail bowl and 'a dozen of Apostle Spoons'. This silver may either have been displayed alongside the best pewter on the parlour dresser, or have stood by itself on the sideboard in the hall, although a few of the

Set of twelve seventeenth-century Apostle spoons from William Hone's Every-Day Book, *published in 1826.*

spoons and candlesticks were probably in daily use, as of course was most of the pewter.

The master bedroom at Berries contained a four-poster bed, some chairs, a toilet table and a chest for clothes. We do not know how the other bedrooms were furnished, but they each probably had several beds in them; a few comfortable feather beds and some low, truckle beds that could be pushed under the big beds out of the way during the daytime.

Elizabeth Winstanley, like her brother William Leader, had always been interested in textiles, and soon after her marriage had opened a draper's shop in Quendon which sold the following materials: 'linen, lawn, calico, tiffany, sarcenet, say, chamlet and shalloon'. She is also known to have been a clever needlewoman with a special fondness for doing embroidery, so it is safe to assume that over the years she stitched many pretty curtains, wall-hangings, quilts and cushion covers for Berries that made the rooms cheerful and bright. William Winstanley, too, loved textiles, and after his mother's death kept on the drapery store, adding 'Velvets and Brocades' to the range of fabrics that she had stocked. His wife would have had many gorgeous stuffs to choose from, therefore, if at any time she wished to replace some of Elizabeth's soft furnishings.

As well as appreciating fine materials, Winstanley was extremely knowledgeable about art, and must have embellished his house with several paintings and engravings. His favourite nephew, Henry Winstanley, the famous artist, inventor and builder of the first rock lighthouse in the world on the treacherous Eddystone reef 14 miles south-west of Plymouth, was a noted landscape painter and etcher. And he probably gave William a few of his framed oil paintings as well as some of his etchings of Audley End, other English country houses and genre prints depicting seventeenth-century daily life. William Winstanley was also a friend of the brilliant etcher Wenceslaus Hollar, and doubtless possessed some examples of his incomparable work.

During the Christmas period the flower garden at the back of Berries, where in summer 'Roses, Gilliflowers, Lavender and Jasmines' grew in profusion, would of course have looked somewhat bare, as would the herb garden, vegetable patch and orchard. The farmyard on the other hand would still have presented a lively scene, with chickens pecking about amongst the cobbles, pigs grunting from their sties, cows in the cow-shed mooing and horses stamping and whinnying in their stable. Winstanley is known to have kept all these animals at Berries after 1670, as well as ducks, geese, pigeons, rabbits, a flock of sheep, a sheep dog, a greyhound for hare-coursing, a little female cat called Puss and several hives of bees. The barn at the side of the farmyard was 'full of corn and straw' and the outhouses of hay.

William Winstanley did not farm quite as much Quendon land as his father; only leasing the fields in the immediate vicinity of Berries such as Dovehouse Field, Mill Field and Kitchen Field, as well as two fields near Quendon Hall. But on these seventy or so acres he grew various root crops, peas, beans, oats, wheat, rye and barley. He did much of the ploughing, sowing and reaping himself, assisted by his servants. After he had performed his daily

*Henry Winstanley's self-portrait of c. 1670,
as it looked in 1918, before it was vandalised and partially restored in 1976.
By courtesey of Saffron Walden Museum.*

stint of writing he found it relaxing to get out into the open air and work in the fields.

From his earliest years William Winstanley had felt a deep affinity, an all-consuming love for Berries, its garden and its 'home' acres. So essential to his happiness had the farm become by the time he was seventeen, in fact, that in the will he made in 1645 his father stipulated that after Elizabeth's death William was to inherit the farm, although by rights it should have gone to his eldest brother Thomas. As Thomas was compensated for the loss of the house by a large sum of money no animosity resulted from this somewhat unfair will and the brothers remained good friends all their lives. In any case, by the time the Quendon property clause came to be implemented in 1670, Thomas was mainly living in London and would not have wanted to move back permanently to Quendon.

When he sold his house in Saffron Walden and took possession of Berries in the summer of 1670, William Winstanley was in the prime of life. Tall and rather thin from his habit of going for long walks and taking constant exercise, he had a distinguished-looking face with an aquiline nose, expressive brown eyes, a neatly clipped moustache and curly brown hair. At this period his family consisted of his second wife Anne, a Cambridge woman whom he had married in 1653, a year after the sudden death of Martha, his son Will, now nineteen and working as a tailor in Quendon, and his daughter Anne, fifteen. In 1678 a second son, Tom, was born, bringing much joy to all the household. The Winstanleys are known to have kept a cook, a maid and a man-

Farmyard scene very like that at Berries;
from Thomas Bewick's History of British Birds,
published in 1797.

servant at Berries, and may also have employed a gardener and
two or three farm labourers.

In his poem *Poor Robin's Perambulation from Saffron Walden to
London*, published in 1678, Mr Winstanley describes Quendon
as 'a little Corporation' possessing 'many a handsome Country-
house', as well as

37

Good air, brave woods, and fine rich Meadow-ground,
And doth with every sort of Grain abound.

There were about thirty families living in Quendon by 1670, ranging from the new Lord of the Manor, Thomas Turner, at Quendon Hall (the Wilfords having left the village by 1645) to several 'poor cotters on the waste'. All these people loved and respected William Winstanley both for his good nature and for his writing ability. His historical works were often read aloud and then minutely discussed at the old King's Head pub in Quendon. But the villagers really liked his *Poor Robin's Almanacks* best. For they always contained a few amusing stories about north-west Essex personalities as well as jokes and Yuletide poems that they could recount to their friends and relations at Christmas. As these almanacs were published in the middle of November each year, the inhabitants of Quendon regarded them as 'Harbingers', announcing the speedy approach of Christmas. And once *Poor Robin's* had made its appearance they felt that it was time to bustle about and prepare in earnest for the festival.

Winstanley tells us that he himself began his Christmas preparations when he spied the first fleet of foreign merchant ships 'come sailing up the River of Thames laden with Prunes and Raisins' some time at the beginning of November. Because he believed in providing lavish hospitality for his guests throughout the Twelve Days of Christmas, stocking up with provisions was of paramount importance to him. So the first thing he and his wife always did to make ready for the festive season was to buy in quantities of groceries.

They had plenty of their own butter, eggs and flour for making Christmas puddings, pies and cakes; honey and rose water to flavour sweets; and dried herbs to add zest to meat. But they needed to purchase 'Raisins, Currants, Dates, Prunes, Figs, Almonds, Sugar, Salt, white and black Pepper, Mustard, Nutmegs, Ginger, Cloves, Cinnamon, Mace, Rice, Tea, Coffee and Chocolatte'. And they knew that they would find all these items in Samuel Leader's grocery emporium in Saffron Walden.

Samuel, the richest man in Walden by 1670, and one of the town's greatest benefactors, was the twin brother of William Leader the mercer, and was even fonder of his nephew William Winstanley than his sibling. He must always have made much of William and Anne when they visited him in his shop, therefore, and was probably particularly assiduous in helping them choose their Christmas groceries.

When William went to Saffron Walden by himself to see his friends and conduct farming business he usually walked there. But when he took his wife in shopping they probably either drove to the town in a light cart or went on horseback, Anne perhaps riding pillion behind William as many farmers' wives did in those days. The road from Quendon to Walden was a very pretty one then, lined with stately oaks and elms until the picturesque village of Newport was reached, and after that climbing steeply up the chalk hills to come out at last into Walden's broad, cobbled High Street with its fine, large merchants' houses, its few select shops and its numerous artisans' dwellings all jumbled up together higgledy-piggledy. Throughout the seventeenth century this

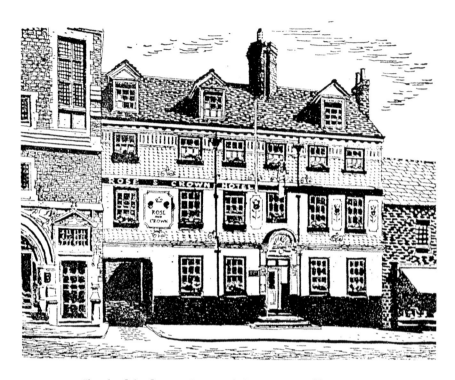

Sketch of the famous Rose and Crown Inn, Saffron Walden,
as it looked in the 1920s.

road had the reputation of being somewhat dangerous to travel on in winter, when it was often deeply rutted and 'miry'. But the Winstanleys were sufficiently familiar with the route to avoid the worst of these hazards and seem never to have had any mishaps.

Before they started their shopping in Walden, the couple put up their horse at the Rose and Crown in the Market Square. This magnificent old coaching inn, for centuries the favourite resort of townsmen and visitors alike, was tragically burnt down in 1969, and today the site is occupied by Boots the chemist.

Samuel Leader's grocery shop was in what is now known as Winstanley House at 4 Market Hill, and in the seventeenth century the shop was surrounded by stables, outbuildings, yards and a large garden. By 1670 Mr Leader had made his fortune and was living just outside Saffron Walden in a vast mansion set in the midst of forty-two acres of land. He no longer had any need to work, therefore, more especially as he was seventy years old, long past the normal retiring age at that time. But he so much enjoyed directing his grocery business, and was such a healthy, active man,

4 Market Hill, Saffron Walden, Samuel Leader's grocery store,
still being used as a shop in 1900. By courtesy of Saffron Walden Museum.

that on most days of the week he was still to be found amongst his numerous assistants in the shop, serving favoured customers himself or taking stock of the goods.

As was usual in seventeenth-century grocery stores most of these goods would have been piled up on trestle tables and on the sturdy wooden counter at one end in boxes, stone jars and metal canisters. Dried fruit was kept loose in wooden drawers under the counter, while whole cheeses, sacks of nuts and grain and other bulky articles stood on the floor. Bunches of herbs hanging from the ceiling would have perfumed the air with their fragrance, which would have mingled enticingly with the more pungent smells of spices, ginger, coffee and tea.

After William and Anne had greeted Samuel Leader, exchanged family gossip with him and perhaps been invited to partake of a little light refreshment in the lovely black-beamed parlour above the shop, they would have begun to place their Christmas order. Some of the smaller items were probably taken away with them there and then, but the greater part of the order would have been delivered to Berries later by waggon or carrier's cart.

As well as food, the couple had to lay in a plentiful supply of wine and spirits with which to regale their guests over the Christmas period. 'Canary, Claret, Malago, Spanish Sack and Rhenish' were William's favourite wines. And he preferred 'Old Nantz Brandy' and 'Cherry Bounce' to any other spirits. These drinks were always ordered from the vintner Thomas Wyatt of Church Street, Saffron Walden.

Although Anne Winstanley may have made some of her candles

at home, extra boxes of wax and tallow candles would also have been needed over the Christmas period. Seventeenth-century householders lit a multiplicity of candles at Yuletide, which was then in fact called 'The Feast of Lights'. The expensive, delicately scented wax candles, probably only used by the Winstanleys on Christmas Day, New Year's Eve and Twelfth Night, may have been bought from Samuel Leader. But the more common tallow candles came from John Gamage's chandler's shop in Little Church Street (now Museum Street).

Having made their various purchases, the Winstanleys generally dined either with William's favourite brother Henry, father of the lighthouse builder, who was a rich mercer-cum-lawyer and by 1670 lived in a large house somewhere on the outskirts of Saffron Walden, or with his closest friend in the town, William Holgate, who owned the lovely sixteenth-century Priory on Common Hill and was a kinsman of the poet Francis Quarles.

If these gentlemen were otherwise engaged, however, William and Anne would have dinner at the Rose and Crown, which William had patronised regularly since his apprentice days and regarded as the finest hostelry in the whole of Essex. He tells us in his *Perambulation* that 'good Sack, good French-Wine, and good Beer' were always to be found there, as well as succulent joints of 'cold roast Beef, or Pork'. He adds that the landlord, Mr Eve, could be relied upon to give his customers 'good words, and reckoning right, without abusage'.

On the first Saturday of November each year a huge fair was held on the Common at Saffron Walden 'for the buying and selling of all manner of Cattle, beasts, goods and merchandise', as Walden's *Mayor's Book* informs us. William Winstanley always attended this fair, both for the purpose of acquiring new livestock and in order to obtain early Christmas presents for his family. Pedlars and tradesmen from London, Cambridge and Bury St Edmunds came to this important fair, bringing with them fashionable clothes, gaily coloured ribbons, toys, books and ballad sheets. And William would go from stall to stall carefully selecting what he thought would please his wife and children most.

Anne appears to have been very fond of 'finery', and in winter wore 'furred gowns', 'close hoods' and natty 'waxed boots'. So William probably often bought her clothes for Christmas – a dress, perhaps, or a lace collar, some stockings or gloves. All these articles would have been of good quality but fairly simple in design, for although William liked rich materials for furnishings he abhorred showiness or ostentation in women's garb, and would not have wished his wife to wear anything too ornate. He himself dressed very plainly, and in his books ridiculed the dandified French fashions for men that came in after the Restoration.

William Winstanley also probably gave his daughter new clothes for Christmas, while for his eldest son he is most likely to have purchased history and poetry books. The boy loved reading as much as his father did, and although he was at first a tailor, he later became a bookseller in Saffron Walden. Winstanley may have bought books for his youngest son, too. A 'Horn-Book' to start with, perhaps, such as Billy, the hero of his famous novel *Sir Billy of Billericay* (published in 1690) was given by his parents,

Lady dressed in furs similar to those worn by Anne Winstanley;
from Wenceslaus Hollar's full-length etching of Winter made in 1644.
By courtesy of the British Museum.

who then went on to buy him 'from a Pedlar's stall at a Fair' several books of folk tales detailing the adventures of characters like 'George and the Dragon, Tom Thumb, Robin Goodfellow, Reynard the Fox and the Knight of the Burning Sword'.

Being exceedingly fond of small children and very indulgent towards them, Winstanley doubtless also showered his baby son, and later his grandsons, with all the toys so beloved of little boys in the seventeenth century – drums, whistles, tin trumpets, wooden swords, balls, marbles, skittles, tops, hobby-horses, paper windmills and kites.

At the Walden November fair William Winstanley purchased items of general interest to the whole family, too. New packs of cards and sets of dice for Christmas games were essential. Everyone liked looking at the latest illustrated broadsheets that recounted the Nativity story. And they all enjoyed old favourite ballads such as 'Fair Rosamund' and 'The Blind Begger of Bethnall Green'.

A great many pedlars brought their wares to the weekly markets held in the Market Square at Walden, and William sometimes did part of his Christmas shopping there as well as at the fair. But if he wanted anything really special he would go up to London and hunt for presents in the shops of the Royal Exchange in Threadneedle Street, where the smartest women's clothes and most ingenious toys in England were to be found. For interesting books he would scour the bookshops in St Paul's Churchyard or on Snow Hill, Holborn. From 1676 to 1698 he kept a newspaper office at the Queen's Head Tavern on Snow Hill, which he visited several times a month, so during those years he would have been able to do more of his Christmas shopping in London.

By the first week in December each year Berries was already well stocked with Christmas provisions, and most of the presents had been bought. Anne Winstanley and her cook now began to concoct the only Christmas delicacy that could be made far in advance – 'Marchpane', a type of rich marzipan sweetmeat, which had been one of Elizabeth Winstanley's specialities and which William and Anne also liked to offer their guests at Yuletide. In those days Christmas

Seventeenth-century hobby-horse seller blowing his trumpet at a fair; from William Hone's Table Book of 1827.

47

cakes and puddings were prepared at the last minute, and the all-important Twelfth cake had by tradition to be so elaborately iced and decorated that it was invariably bought ready-made from a confectioner.

From 1670 onwards the cookery book chiefly used by William and Anne was Hannah Woolley's *The Queene-Like Closet or Rich Cabinet*, which came out that year. Hannah Woolley (or Wolley), the Mrs Beeton of her day, had been born somewhere in Essex in 1623, and in 1647 had married Benjamin Woolley, the Master of Newport Grammar School and an acquaintance of the Quendon Winstanleys. Already by that date Hannah was an accomplished cook, physician and needlewoman. She had much in common with Elizabeth Winstanley, therefore, who befriended the young woman and taught her quite a bit of additional cookery and herb lore.

When the Woolleys left Newport in 1653 to start a school of their own in Hackney, they kept in touch with the Winstanleys. It was probably William who encouraged Hannah to publish her first book in 1661. Certainly he mentioned all her cookery books in his almanacs and newspapers, but especially recommended *The Queene-Like Closet*, which contains recipes for many of the Essex Winstanleys' favourite dishes, some of which may actually have been given to Hannah by Elizabeth. The instructions for preparing 'Marchpane' to be found in *The Closet*, together with recipes for most of the other Christmas fare enjoyed by the Winstanleys, appear on pages 141–46 of the present book.

While Anne Winstanley was busily employed in making

THE
QUEENE-LIKE CLOSET
Or
RICH   CABINET

Frontispiece
to Hannah
Woolley's
Queene-Like
Closet or
Rich Cabinet
of 1670.
By courtesy
of the British
Library.

Printed for Rich: Lownes
the White Lion in Duck Layne neare West Smithfield 1670.

sweets, William brewed several gallons of spiced ale, sorted out his best apples, pears and nuts for Christmas eating and brought down to the kitchen the finest bunches of dried sage, thyme and marjoram to flavour Yuletide pies and roasts. He always retained his boyhood interest in herbal remedies, and every Christmas made a delectable cough linctus of 'Hysop, Gum Dragon and white sugar Candy' in case any of his family or guests caught a chill during the holiday.

In the middle of December a great cleaning operation started at Berries. The mats and carpets were beaten, the furniture was polished with beeswax, the pewter rubbed until it 'shone like Silver' and the beds in the spare bedrooms were made up and thoroughly aired with warming-pans.

Every November William Winstanley killed several of his pigs, which were 'straight into Bacon made'. But he also killed another pig in December to eat at Christmas. One or two sheep were killed in December, too, and in some years an ox, although he generally bought his Christmas beef from a butcher in Saffron Walden. William's turkeys came from a Walden poulterer, but he killed his own chickens, capons, ducks and geese as required over the Christmas period. The successive Earls of Suffolk and owners of Quendon Hall always presented the Winstanleys with venison at Christmas. And the countless pheasants, partridges, teal, widgeon and mallards that the family consumed over the holiday may either have been gifts from friends and patrons or have been shot by William himself, who we know also went hare-coursing.

On 21st December Anne Winstanley always got down to her

first major session of Christmas cooking. For the next three days 'such boyling and broyling, such roasting and toasting, such stewing and brewing, such baking, frying, cutting and slashing' took place in the kitchen at Berries as 'greatly rejoiced' the hospitable heart of William Winstanley, and made him glad that he had married a woman who was just as skilful a cook as his mother had been.

During these days numerous rich fruit cakes, plum puddings and traditional 'white Christmas loaves' (small round milk loaves about the size of cricket balls) were made, as well as sausages, brawn, pigeon pies, venison pasties, tubs of clotted cream and dozens and dozens of mince pies.

By the evening of 23rd December all this food lay neatly arranged 'on the Pantry shelves'. And knowing that the most laborious of the Christmas culinary tasks had now been completed, Anne would have been able to relax and, like William and the children, begin to look forward to the arrival of their guests and the start of the Christmas holidays on the morrow.

CHRISTMAS EVE

THROUGHOUT the period that William and Anne lived at Berries, the farm continued to be the Christmas gathering place of the entire Essex Winstanley clan, just as it had always been in Elizabeth's day. Actually staying in the house over the whole Yuletide holidays would usually be William's brother Henry accompanied by his wife Anne and their two youngest daughters Dorothy and Arabella, and their youngest son Charles with his wife Penelope and their five children from Saffron Walden, Henry's eldest son, Henry the lighthouse builder, and his wife Elizabeth, and Henry senior's daughter Susan, her husband Benjamin Newbolt and their son Henry from Littlebury, Henry senior's middle son Robert and his wife Martha from Henham, and William's sister Mary, her husband John Smart and their son John from Theydon Bois.

All the remaining members of the Winstanley family lived within easy walking distance of the farm, and simply joined in the merrymaking whenever they wished. William's brother Thomas and his wife Elizabeth owned a cottage next to the King's Head in Quendon, to which they returned for Christmas every year from London. His youngest brother James, a tanner, lived on Rickling Green with his wife Joanna and their son James. And his widowed sister Anne Perry lived at Rickling with her six children. By 1670 William's two other sisters were dead. Susan had remained single. Elizabeth had married Thomas Humphrey, who helped the Winstanleys run the farm at Berries, and he and his six children were some of William and Anne's most welcome guests.

Several of Anne Winstanley's relatives from Cambridge may also have stayed at Berries over Christmas, as may a few of the many cousins that the Winstanleys are believed to have had in London. Their numerous Leader cousins in Saffron Walden and Nightingale cousins in Newport had standing invitations to visit Berries at any time they liked during the Twelve Days of Christmas. So did a whole host of families with whom the Winstanleys had long been intimate in Walden – Gamages, Holgates, Meritons, Barons, Felbridges, Archers, Parkers and Waites. In Quendon itself the Winstanleys' particular friends were the Knights, who rented a large farm near the church, the Jacksons, who lived next door to them, and the Greens, who lived in a house on the edge of Quendon Wood. These families, too, were cordially invited to take part in all the Winstanleys' Christmas junketings.

Most of the house guests arrived at Berries in time for midday dinner on Christmas Eve and left on 7th January. Christmas was the only real holiday they had in the year, so they liked to extract as much enjoyment from it as they could and make it last as long as possible. But if business pressed they sometimes only reached the farm on Christmas Day and departed on New Year's Eve.

Dinner was always held early on Christmas Eve, for in the afternoon a great holly-gathering expedition was made to Quendon Wood, and William liked the party to set off in good time. This first Yuletide meal was a pleasant, informal affair, with guests simply helping themselves from the huge dishes of ham, brawn, cold sausages, venison pasties, pigeon pies, game pies and mince pies that were laid out on the table in the hall, and washing the food down with copious draughts of William's home-made cider, perry, spiced ale or extra-strong Christmas beer.

Winstanley tells us that 'tongues wagged fast and furious' as everyone caught up with family news. He himself went from group to group, greeting newcomers, cracking jokes, filling up mugs and tankards, and repeatedly urging his friends and relatives not to stint themselves but to 'eat right heartily' of all the 'fine victuals' his wife had prepared for them. In general William believed that people should be 'moderate in their drink and diet', and he strongly condemned both drunkenness and gluttony. But at Christmas he liked to supply his guests with an abundance of good things and to watch them feasting merrily.

Large game pie flanked by a pigeon pie and some mince pies.

As soon as the meal was over all the men and boys and sometimes a few of the womenfolk donned 'warm coats' or 'hooded
cloaks' and sallied forth to pick Christmas greenery in Quendon
Wood. In those days the wood was a dense forest of oaks, hazels,
hornbeams and beech trees. But then as now it was criss-crossed
with paths which periodically emerged into a glade or clearing.
Mr Winstanley tells us that in one of these glades 'in the Heart
of the Wood' there was a small cluster of holly trees from which
he always cut his holly branches. To William holly, with its glossy
green leaves and scarlet berries, seemed the very epitome of
Yuletide mirth, and it was undoubtedly his favourite Christmas
decoration. However, he also quite liked 'the pretty, clinging Ivy'.
So after he and his party had picked a cart-load of holly they
placed on top several long strands of ivy 'to twine about Posts and
Banisters' at the farm. Then home they trudged in the gathering
dusk; sometimes along frozen tracks, sometimes through snow,
singing songs like the following ditty composed by William
Winstanley in 1667 to keep their spirits up:

Now Christmas is come,
Let us beat up the Drum,
And call all our Neighbours together.
And when they appear,
Let us make them such chear
As will keep out the wind and the weather.

While the holly-gatherers were busy in Quendon Wood,
Anne Winstanley and the friends who had stayed behind with

Sketch of a hanging garland
copied from an engraving of 1675.

her picked sprigs of bay, laurel and rosemary in the garden at
Berries to add variety to the Christmas decorations. Mistletoe
was not used as a kissing-bough until the eighteenth century and
although some seventeenth-century families included the plant
in their Yuletide decorations the Winstanleys never appear to
have done so. After all the pictures, mirrors, mantelpieces and
sideboards of the house had been 'plentifully adorned' with
greenery they may, however, have fashioned the remaining twigs
of holly, bay and rosemary into a hanging garland, the precursor

of the kissing-bough, which was usually suspended over the dining-table in parlour or hall.

To reward his guests for their help in cutting greenery and decorating the farm, William Winstanley always provided an especially lavish supper on Christmas Eve; a typical main course being 'Roast Pheasants and Partridges, Quails, a dish of Larks, Shoulders of Mutton, Legs of Pork, Turnips and potato pies'. Unlike most seventeenth-century families the Winstanleys were extremely fond of vegetables and ate a lot of them. Carrots, onions, leeks, parsnips, cabbages and dried peas featured daily on their menus throughout the winter months, but the rare and more costly potatoes were only served up on special occasions.

For dessert at supper on Christmas Eve there was usually 'a Trifle' or 'a whipt Sillibub' as well as mince pies and clotted cream. Winstanley considered mince pies to be 'the most delectable Dainties ever invented', and partook of one or two at every meal throughout the Twelve Days of Christmas. He thought them 'good hot and good cold', but best of all when smothered in the excellent 'clouted cream' that his wife was so adept at making.

A selection of William Winstanley's choicest wines accompanied the food. And he gallantly drank toasts to all the ladies present, saying as he did so, 'Madam, I pledge ye and bid ye welcome', or 'I drink to your health, Madam, and pray ye be merry'.

After everyone had eaten and drunk their fill, they rose from the table and grouped themselves about the inglenook fireplace in the hall. In his almanacs Winstanley frequently describes the 'blazing' fires 'heaped high with Logs' that he had at Berries over

Christmas, but he never mentions burning a specific Yule log. We must assume, therefore, that the Winstanleys did not subscribe to this custom. It would appear, indeed, that although the Yule log was an important feature of the Christmas festivities in the North of England and the West Country throughout the seventeenth century, it was not very common in the Eastern Counties. As William believed that 'keeping up good hot Fires' was one of the most essential duties of a host at Christmas time, we can be certain, however, that even without a Yule log the huge fireplace in the hall at Berries glowed exceedingly brightly all during the holidays.

And never did the flames leap higher, perhaps, than on the night of Christmas Eve. For annually from 1670 to 1698 the Winstanleys held a grand fireside ceilidh on this night to which all their friends, neighbours and servants were invited as well as the whole family. The main object of the gathering was to sing carols and tell stories, but there was always a little impromptu dancing, too, and much feasting and merrymaking. All in all it was a very enjoyable occasion and one that nobody ever wanted to miss.

When the house guests had chatted and rested awhile after supper, they assisted the Winstanleys in their preparations for the party. And by the time the first of the evening visitors started to arrive at Berries at about nine o'clock, the long hall table had been pushed to one side, and all the benches, chairs and stools in the house arranged in a semicircle round the fire. 'A caldron of Mull'd Sack' simmered gently on the hob, and near the hearth

*Engraving of c. 1800, showing a farmhouse hall
on Christmas Eve, with mummers and musicians.*

stood a low table completely covered with jugs of spiced ale, beer, cider and perry, great slabs of fruit cake, plates of mince pies and venison pasties and numerous little dishes of marchpane and honey sweets. What with all this festive fare, the attractive evergreen decorations, the burnished pewter and silver glinting in the candlelight and the roaring log fire surrounded by 'a happy, jovial company', the hall must have presented a supremely welcoming appearance to those entering it from the cold darkness without. And after being conducted to a fireside seat and plied with refreshments, the newcomers soon warmed up and began eagerly to look forward to the forthcoming entertainments.

Henry Winstanley, the inventor, made musical boxes, barrel-organs and automata in his spare time, and at Christmas brought a few of these delightful toys over to Berries to keep the company amused while they waited for all the guests to assemble on Christmas Eve and other party nights. He was proficient at reading and writing music, and may have played ordinary instruments as well as mechanical ones. But if Henry was unable to strike up a tune on the flute or violin, there was always someone in William's entourage who could, for, as he mentions in his almanacs, he numbered several 'fiddlers and pipers' from Saffron Walden and Bishops Stortford, Hertfordshire, amongst his friends. As music to accompany dancing or singing was of vital importance to the Winstanleys, one or other of them would certainly have been in attendance at Berries throughout the festive season.

All the Essex Winstanleys were passionately fond of dancing, so before the carol-singing and story-telling began they would doubtless have executed a few of the lively jigs, reels and circle dances that were so popular at that time in country districts. Exhausted by their efforts, family and guests would then have returned to the fireside, piled on more logs and replenished their mugs and plates.

Young Will might then have opened the carol concert by singing one of his father's Christmas lyrics, which were apparently often 'sung to the tune of a fiddle'. He was very proud of William Winstanley's writings and is said to have had a good clear voice.

Since the 1820s a great many of William's Yuletide poems have regularly been included in Christmas anthologies, and are thus fairly well known. The best loved, however, is his 'Christmas Song' of 1695, which runs as follows:

Now thrice welcome Christmas,
Which brings us good Chear,
Minc'd Pies and plumb Porridge,
Good Ale and strong Bear;
With Pig, Goose and Capon,
The best that may be,
So well doth the Weather
And our Stomachs agree.

Observe how the Chimneys
Do smoak all about,
The Cooks are providing
For Dinner no doubt;
But those on whose Table
No Victuals appear,
O may they keep Lent
All the rest of the Year.

With Holly and Ivy
So green and so gay,
We deck up our Houses
As fresh as the day;

With Bays and Rosemary,
And Lawrel compleat,
And every one now
Is a King in conceit.

Next to dancing, the 'singing of jolly carols' was the Winstanleys' favourite Christmas occupation, and at the ceilidh on Christmas Eve they went through virtually the entire repertoire of seventeenth-century carols with great verve and gusto. William Winstanley may have owned a copy of the first carol book to appear in England, which was printed by Wynkyn de Worde in 1521. He much admired this printer's work, and was always on the look-out for examples of it. Certainly he possessed de Worde's *Martyrology* and *New Testament*, so probably he had his carols, too. Further collections of carols came out in 1550, 1611, 1642, 1661 and 1688. By the 1660s the words and music of individual carols were also printed as broadsheets and hawked about by pedlars.

Several of the carols that are popular today were already well known in the seventeenth century, including 'The Boar's Head Carol', 'The Holly and the Ivy', 'I Saw Three Ships', 'God Rest Ye Merry, Gentlemen' and 'The First Nowell'. Other carols that were often sung then but are rarely heard nowadays were 'The Cherry Tree Carol', 'Welcome Yule' and 'Tomorrow Shall Be My Dancing Day'.

After the carol-singing more refreshments were served, and then everyone drew their chairs yet closer round the hearth and waited in breathless expectation for the story-telling session to begin. At that time William Winstanley was reputed to be the finest story-teller in the land, and to sit in flickering firelight listening to the spell-binding tales that he delivered in his deep, melodious voice must have been a truly wonderful experience. The guests who attended his Christmas Eve parties certainly thought so, and always insisted that he should be the chief narrator at the ceilidhs. Being a polite, considerate host, Winstanley never started the story-telling himself, however, but would call on one or other of his visitors to set the ball rolling.

William's eldest brother Thomas held some position in the Lord Chamberlain's Office throughout the 1670s, and in the 1680s was connected with the Yeomen of the Guard, so he knew much about what went on at Charles II's dissolute Court and doubtless told many fascinating anecdotes about the King and his mistresses. Henry Winstanley made the Grand Tour of Europe in the early 1670s, so must have had several exciting traveller's tales to narrate after his return in 1674. And when he became Clerk of the Works to Charles II at the then Royal Palaces of Audley End and Newmarket in 1679, he, too, would have had much to tell about Court life. And William's farmer friend, John Knight, was a merry, waggish extrovert who was acquainted with almost everyone in north-west Essex, and always had a stock of amusing stories about his fellow county men, which he would have been only too pleased to relate to the company on Christmas Eve.

At the urgent request of his friends and relatives, from the late 1670s onwards, William Winstanley always began his own part of the Christmas Eve entertainment by repeating the story of his encounter with a highwayman – a thrilling tale that for them never palled. The highwayman in question was Jack Bird, 'a notorious Malefactor', who was eventually hanged at Tyburn in 1690. And as William was walking along a lonely stretch of road near Waltham Abbey one day in 1678, the mounted robber suddenly emerged from behind a bush and, covering him with a pistol, ordered him to 'Stand and deliver!' Quite unafraid, Winstanley jested with Bird, thanking him for the compliment he paid him in thinking that he, the author Poor Robin, would carry anything worth stealing, and adding that in all fairness the highwayman. ought to let him off scot-free, as he had immortalised several of his comrades, including Claude Duval, by recounting their exploits in his almanacs. This banter did not mollify Jack Bird, however, who stole fifteen shillings from Winstanley, as well as his new hat.

'Now, sir', said Bird, 'I have given you cause to immortalise me, too.'

'Yes', replied Winstanley, 'for a rogue, sir.'

Also popular with William Winstanley's guests were his accounts of the crazy, surrealistic voyages that his friend and mentor, John Taylor, the 'Water Poet', had embarked on in his youth; the most extraordinary of which took place in July 1619, when he had rowed down the Thames from London to Queenborough in Kent in a 'browne-paper boat' equipped with oars fashioned from 'Stock-fishes unbeaten, bound fast to two canes with pack-thread'.

William himself was very interested in the strange and bizarre and wrote much surrealistic prose. To amuse the children, who were always allowed to stay up on Christmas Eve, he would then go on to describe his imaginary, surrealistic kingdom, 'Lubberland', where the people lived in houses built of 'venison-pasty crust', the mountains were made of 'Parmezan grated cheese', the rocks were 'sugar-candy' and the rivers 'ebbed and flowed with pure Canary'. Dotted about the countryside were 'Minced-pie trees', upon whose branches perched 'ready-roasted capons'. And beneath the trees lay piles of logs made from 'Westphalia hams of Bacon'.

Next, Winstanley might recount the quixotic adventures of his fictitious hero, Sir Billy of Billericay, 'the last Knight Errant in England', who rode about Essex on his trusty steed Belerophon, tilting at scarecrows instead of windmills, fighting giants and rescuing princesses from wicked magicians.

This stirring tale was usually followed by the no less riveting story of the famous 'Basilisk or Cockatrice', which 'in former time lurked about the Meads near Saffron Walden', and 'by his very sight, killed so many as the Town became depopulated'. One day, however, 'a valorous Knight' dressed in a 'Coat of Christal Glass' went off to fight the cockatrice. In the event he had no need to attack, for as soon as the 'venomous Serpent' was confronted by the dazzling brightness of the knight's coat, it promptly fell down dead.

A tablet setting out all the details of this adventure was subsequently hung up in Saffron Walden Church, but Mr Winstanley tells us that during the Civil War the plaque was considered to be

Heraldic cockatrice.

'a monument to superstition', and was 'by the lawless Souldiers broken in pieces, to show they were also of a venomous Nature as well as the Cockatrice'.

After this would come a spate of marvellous stories about dragons, ogres, witches and wizards, happy young lovers, chivalrous kings, some of which were taken from Shakespeare or Chaucer, others from English ballads or folk lore. Then Winstanley would move on to fairy tales and describe the pranks of Robin Goodfellow or the 'wanton Gambols' of Queen Mab and her train.

By now at Berries it would be growing late; the chimes of midnight not far off, when the Eve of Christmas turned into the hallowed Day itself. But before that moment came and the party ended, William Winstanley always wound up the proceedings by narrating the Nativity story – that wondrous tale about 'the Babe and his Mother, the lowly stable, the Three Wise Men and the Star', which seemed to him 'the most beautiful Story ever written'.

Seventeenth-century woodcut of the Nativity, from William Hone's Every-Day Book, *1826.*

CHRISTMAS DAY

WILLIAM WINSTANLEY believed that Christmas Day, 'the Birthday of the God of Love', should be celebrated by showing loving kindness to the whole of creation. The first thing he himself always did 'on the morn of this Golden Day of Days' was to visit all his farm animals in turn and bestow on each one a Christmas greeting and an extra ration of food. He wanted the garden birds to share in the general Yuletide rejoicings, too, and for them he put out a liberal allowance of crumbs and titbits. We may be sure that his sheepdog, his greyhound and the little cat, Puss, who he tells us spent most of the winter curled up in front of the parlour fire, were not forgotten either, but probably received some tasty meat scraps and bowls of cream on Christmas Day.

Throughout the winter months Winstanley permitted tramps and beggars to sleep in his barn. If any of these men occupied the barn on Christmas Eve they were doubtless given supper that night as well as a hearty breakfast on Christmas morning.

After William had fed his animals, and perhaps wished the tramps and his farm labourers the compliments of the season, it

*Feeding
cattle
on
Christmas
morning.*

would be time for him to preside over his guests' Christmas-Day breakfast. He and his family always ate a good old-fashioned English breakfast of cold meat, cold pie, boiled eggs or Cheshire cheese washed down with ale, beer or 'a comfortable caudle'. But to please their guests at Christmas time, he and Anne added barrels of oysters, toast and honey, tea, coffee and chocolate to the breakfast menu. Winstanley considered tea to be 'nothing but dish-water', and he called coffee 'Ninny-broth'. But over the holiday period he kept these opinions to himself. For his only criterion then was politeness to his visitors, and he knew that several of them were very partial to these 'newfangled' drinks.

No presents appeared at the breakfast table on Christmas Day at Berries because in the seventeenth century the exchange of gifts always took place on New Year's Day. Many warm hugs and kisses were given all round, however, for the Winstanleys were a demonstrative family and liked to show their affection for one another in this way. Perhaps taking after their father, Henry, who had doted on Elizabeth, William and his brothers appear, indeed, to have been exceptionally uxorious; not only appreciating their wives as compliant bedfellows but respecting them for their various talents and abilities. In his almanacs William Winstanley urges his readers to 'make much of your wives and treat them kindly'. He adds that on cold winter nights

There's nothing like to keep you warm,
As loving wife laid in your arm.

Breakfast over, Anne Winstanley retired to the kitchen to

POOR ROBINS

Hue and Cry

AFTER
GOOD HOUSE-KEEPING.

OR,

A DIALOGUE
BETWIXT

𝕲𝖔𝖔𝖉 𝕳𝖔𝖚𝖘𝖊=𝕶𝖊𝖊𝖕𝖎𝖓𝖌, 𝕮𝖍𝖗𝖎𝖘𝖙𝖒𝖆𝖘, and 𝕻𝖗𝖎𝖉𝖊.

Shewing how *Good House-Keeping* is grown out of Date both in City and Country, and *Christmas* become only a meer name, and not to be found by Feasting in Gentlemens Houses, but only by Red-Letters in *Almanacks.* And how the Money that should go to Feast the Poor at *Christmas* is spent upon the maintenance of *Pride*, with how many Trades are maintained by *Pride*, and how many undone for want of *Good House-Keeping.*

Good House-Keeping *is Banished,*
And Pride *is come up in its stead.*

This may be Printed,
Dec. 17.1687. *R. P.*

LONDON,
Printed for *Randal Taylor*, near *Stationers-Hall*, 1687.

assist her cook and maid in preparing dishes for the all-important Christmas dinner, which would be served up at about one
o'clock. 'Caldrons, Frying-Pans, Dripping-Pans, Kettles, Gridirons'
and various other 'necessary utensils belonging to Good-
Housekeeping' were now used to their full capacity, as William
informs us, adding that 'the Jack' now began 'to play musick and
the spits to turn round to it'.

This was the sort of music that Winstanley considered ought
to be heard in every gentleman's kitchen on Christmas Day,
when, in his view, it was 'the bounden duty' of the rich to feast
their 'needy neighbours' and 'afford them good cheer'. He annually repeated this message in his newspaper and almanacs, and in
1687 decided to write an entire book on the subject, his famous
Poor Robins Hue and Cry after Good House-Keeping. This forceful work,
a passionate plea to the Nation to bring back our traditional
English Christmas, with its lavish hospitality and unstinting
generosity to the poor, made a deep impression on the populace
and finally succeeded in bringing about that widespread revival
of interest in the festival which the author had long been striving
to effect.

Divine Service always played an important part in the
Winstanleys' Christmas celebrations. Soon after breakfast on
Christmas Day, William, who was churchwarden of Quendon
Church, would walk over to the church along the wide, grassy
slype that led directly from his garden to the churchyard to
check that everything was in order for Matins. On one side
of the slype lay the rectory garden; on the other Winstanley's

own Dovehouse Field. And every time he went along this path he usually took careful note of how his crops were progressing. On Christmas morning, however, his thoughts were doubtless focused more on the service he was about to attend than on his winter wheat. For him the Feast of the Nativity was 'the most blithesome' day of the year, and he longed to join the rest of the congregation in pouring out thanks to God for the birth of their Saviour. The following short poem that he wrote in December, 1681, seems perfectly to express his Yuletide feelings:

This month the King of Kings was born,
Who did Salvation bring.
Then let us all rejoyce therefore,
And praises to him sing.

The earliest picture of Quendon Church that has yet come to light is a rough sketch executed by a Mr Thomas Bird of Romford in 1734. This drawing depicts the church as a small, barn-like structure with a south porch, three arches in the south wall, which had been bricked in some time during the sixteenth century when the south aisle was demolished, a tiled roof and a squat wooden belfry at the west end, housing a single bell. The building probably looked very similar in the seventeenth century, but was altered out of all recognition in 1861 when a new roof and south aisle were constructed. Plain as it was, William Winstanley loved this little thirteenth-century church dearly, and at Christmas did everything he could to embellish the interior. He provided wax candles for the altar out of his own pocket, gave the parish clerk a generous amount of holly, ivy and garden greenery with which to decorate the church, and sent one of his servants to fetch the flowers and special evergreen sprays that the Lords of the Manor always contributed.

In the seventeenth century the inside walls of Quendon Church were whitewashed and had sentences of Scripture written upon them in large, black letters. The nave contained several oak box pews as well as ordinary pews, a wooden pulpit and an octagonal stone font. As the windows were more numerous in those days, the building would always have been flooded with light.

When Winstanley unlocked the doors of the church on Christmas morning it must have looked very festive with the candles and flowers on the altar and the greenery wreathed about the pulpit and pews. As he walked up and down the church, setting out the silver chalice, Bible and prayer books needed for the service, he must have enjoyed the aromatic, quintessentially Christmassy scent of the candles and evergreens to the full. He delighted in all manner of perfumes, and testing the rose, lavender and Hungary waters that he distilled at Berries had given him a discerning sense of smell.

Shortly after Mr Winstanley had opened the church, the bell-ringer and the rector would have arrived. William makes no mention of any of the three rectors – Job Aye, Francis Hutchinson and Henry Trussleton – who ministered at Quendon between 1670 and 1698. But as he remained churchwarden during all these years we may assume that he was on good terms with them. Next, the

*Present-day Quendon Church, with original porch and exterior walls,
but Victorian roof and modern belfry.*

congregation would have filed into church, and the Christmas
Day service could then begin.

There was no organ in Quendon Church in the seventeenth
century, but there may have been a couple of violins or some
other instruments to accompany the singing of the psalms and
carols. Even without music, however, the Winstanleys would
have been sure to sing lustily on this joyful morning, their jubi-
lant voices expressing the great love for Christ that they felt in
their hearts.

After Matins the Winstanleys greeted their friends in the church porch, wishing them all 'a very merry Christmas'. A few of these friends and several of the poorer villagers were always invited to Christmas dinner at Berries, and William and Anne would soon have hurried off home to prepare for their guests.

Because of the large number of people who needed to be accommodated for Christmas dinner, one or two trestle tables would be placed at the end of the table in the hall at Berries to form 'a single long board'. William Winstanley tells us that 'the cloth was then laid, the trenchers spread, the bread placed, the napkins displaid and the salt-cellar fixt'. When all the guests were seated Winstanley said grace, 'the dishes marched up piping hot' and everyone 'fell to'.

At the Winstanleys' Christmas dinner the first course was always frumenty, a sort of thick porridge containing wheat or pearl barley, eggs, cream, sugar and spice. Next to mince pies, frumenty, or furmity as he also sometimes calls it, was William's favourite Christmas delicacy, and from Christmas Day onwards a bowl of the mixture, cold, generally stood on the sideboard in the hall for visitors to help themselves to.

A vast joint of 'Roast-Beef' held pride of place at the top of the table during the meat course. But for those who preferred poultry there were turkeys, geese, ducks, capons and chickens. Rich sauces accompanied the meat, as well as potato pies and the special white Christmas loaves. To amuse the children Winstanley sometimes made one of these warm loaves 'dance on the table' by placing a quill full of 'Quicksilver' inside it. He knew a great many

Christmas dinner at Bracebridge Hall,
based on descriptions of William Winstanley's own Yuletide feast at Berries;
from Randolph Caldicott's Old Christmas *of 1875.*

conjuring tricks, several of which he would perform on Christmas afternoon, but this was the only trick he demonstrated at dinner. Throughout the meal, however, he kept the whole company in a roar with the jokes, riddles and funny stories that he told, and the hall echoed and re-echoed 'with joyous laughter'.

Mince pies and 'Plumb-Pudding' followed the main course. And towards the end of dessert the manservant would set down on the table William Winstanley's silver wassail bowl filled with 'Lambs-Wool', a potent concoction composed of 'Nut-brown Ale', spices and sugar, with baked apples and pieces of toast floating on top. We are not told what Winstanley's bowl looked like, but seventeenth-century silver wassail bowls were usually very ornate and had cherubs' heads, cartouches, curlicues and arabesques engraved all over them. As everyone took a sip from the bowl, turn and turn about, a number of lively drinking songs were sung, including William's own charming 'Wassail Song' written in 1681. It runs as follows:

Victorian engraving of a seventeenth-century silver wassail bowl.

> The brown bowle,
> The merry brown bowle,
> As it goes round about a
> Fill,
> Still,
> Let the world say what it will,
> And drink your drink all out a.

The deep Canne,
The merry deep Canne,
As thou doest freely quaffe a,
Sing,
Fling,
Be as merry as a King,
And sound a lusty laugh a.

Healths were then drunk to the King, to absent friends and to one another. And when the bowl was at last empty, the company removed to the fireside, where comfortably ensconced by the cheerful blaze they savoured glasses of Winstanley's 'Cherry-Bounce' and 'Old Nantz Brandy', nibbled marchpane and smoked their pipes.

When his guests had had time to digest their Christmas dinner, William, to whom fresh air and exercise were very important, would propose a walk, some outdoor games, or, in frosty weather, the Winstanleys' favourite sport of all – skating. From the diary of John Evelyn and other contemporary sources we learn that in Southern England snow fell and ponds froze over during the Christmas period in 1673, 1676, 1681, 1683, 1684, 1688, 1694, 1695 and 1696. So the Winstanleys would have been able to enjoy quite a bit of skating in the years that William and Anne lived at Berries, and doubtless made the most of their opportunities.

As previously mentioned, the large pond at the bottom of the garden at Berries (called Kitchen Pond as it extended into neighbouring Kitchen Field) made an ideal skating rink in winter,

Etching of 1787, showing skaters on a pond.

and it was here that the Winstanleys practised the sport. Today Kitchen Pond is hidden by undergrowth and has almost totally dried up. But from the seventeenth century until about 1920 it was a beautiful sheet of water fringed only by a few willow trees. And on those Christmas afternoons long ago when William and his party disported themselves here on the ice, the pond must have presented a delightful scene of animation, with men, women and children 'skimming merrily' hither and thither and 'laughing with glee'. Winstanley tells us that 'when night began to encroach on the day' the group returned to the house tired but happy and seated themselves round the hall fire again, where they recounted their several skating feats and adventures.

In mild winters, when Kitchen Pond did not freeze, the Winstanleys and their adult friends would go for a walk through Quendon Wood or along the lanes outside the village on Christmas afternoon. Meanwhile the little girls played 'tag' and 'hide-and-seek' in the garden at Berries, and the boys set off on the exciting cross-country run known as 'Shoeing the Wild Mare'. In this popular seventeenth-century game, which seems only to have been played at Christmas time, one boy, the 'Wild Mare', was allowed a certain start, after which his companions gave chase. If the 'Mare' managed to outstrip his pursuers and return to base he won the game. But if he was caught, he was thrown to the ground and shod with imaginary horseshoes.

At dusk the children would troop back indoors, where Anne Winstanley regaled them with 'warm possets', cakes and sweet-meats. William would then organise some games for them in the hall. He loved children and understood them well, never patronising them as most seventeenth-century adults tended to do, but taking a genuine interest in their concerns, and when playing with them entering fully into the spirit of whatever game was in progress. With his ready smile, twinkling brown eyes and irrepressible sense of fun, the young considered him, indeed, to be the ideal playmate and were always eager for his company.

William Winstanley tells us that the games played in the hall at Berries on Christmas Day were 'Hoodman Blind, Hot Cockles, Hunt the Slipper and Stool-Ball'. The first of these was a sort of Blind Man's Buff where one person had a hood put over his head or a scarf tied round his eyes and then had to run about the room trying to catch the others. In Hot Cockles a blindfolded child laid his head in another's lap and his companions came up and tapped him on the shoulder one by one until he correctly guessed who it was. For Hunt the Slipper a group of boys and girls would sit in a circle on the floor and quickly pass a slipper from one to the other under their doublets and pinafores, while one child outside the ring tried to guess who had it. There appear to have been several versions of Stool-Ball in the seventeenth century, some to be played out of doors, some indoors. In a popular variant of the indoor game a stool would be placed in the middle of the room and a child chosen to stand guard over it. Armed with soft balls or small cushions the other children would then try to hit the stool, while the guardian attempted to deflect the missiles with his hands and feet.

After the games it would be time for William's display of conjuring. This was mainly intended to amuse the youngsters, but probably attracted several grown-ups, too. It may have been held in the parlour, where he would have had a chance to prepare his hocus-pocus unobserved, or perhaps in a quiet corner of the hall. To dazzle his audience, Winstanley would open the show with a series of brilliant card tricks in which he always guessed correctly which cards the children had hidden in the pack. Then he would make coins 'suddenly appear' and just as suddenly 'Vanish clean away'. At a tap of his magic wand an egg would 'stand on its Head' or an apple 'move about the table of itself'. And he was expert at the old dodge of seeming to pour a gallon of liquid into a pint pot. He invariably ended the entertainment by demonstrating his famous 'Candle that burns under water'. And when he lit the wick and plunged the candle into a pail of water, and still the little flame continued to burn steady, the children's wonder and delight knew no bounds.

We are not told what the Winstanleys ate for supper on Christmas Day. But after their gargantuan dinner it was probably something light. William often says that he thinks 'cold Gammon of Bacon stuft with cloves' makes a tasty snack at Christmas time when eaten with bread and butter. So the family may have supped off one of these hams, a cold pigeon pie, some cold chicken and turkey and a barrel or two of oysters. Winstanley was very fond of oysters as a supper dish, especially when accompanied by 'a glass of good Sack'. As well as eating more vegetables than the average seventeenth-century family, the Winstanleys also consumed more fruit. And for dessert on Christmas night they may have had baked apples and cream, one of Anne's delicious 'Warden pies' (pies made from warden pears) and a selection of fresh fruit, including apples and pears from the garden and 'filberds' picked in Quendon Wood.

More lambswool circulated after supper, now served in the traditional small brown wooden wassail bowls that were easier to pass from hand to hand than the large silver bowl, which seems only to have been used at Christmas dinner, and on New Year's Eve and Twelfth Night. Winstanley may also have mixed some punch on the evening of Christmas Day. There is a recipe for punch in Hannah Woolley's *Queene-Like Closet*, which lists the ingredients as wine, brandy, nutmeg, sugar and lemon juice. And by the 1670s this drink had already become an extremely popular Yuletide beverage in England.

Having enjoyed a few bumpers of lambswool or punch, the poor villagers who had been invited to spend Christmas Day with the Winstanleys would take their leave. For, although earnestly pressed to stay on by William and Anne, they believed that the family should be allowed a little time to themselves, and apparently always went home after supper.

There then remained round the hall fire an intimate party of relatives and close friends, who for a while would just sip their drinks, smoke their pipes and talk companionably together. After a time a fiddler or a piper might begin to play a carol, when at once everyone would burst into song. Then, almost impercep-tibly, the music would change from a lilting carol melody to a 'lively dance tune'. Up would jump first one couple and then an-other, until very soon the room would be full of leaping, twirling figures, all gaily treading the measure of a country dance.

The Winstanleys and their friends preferred the 'simple old Dances' of the English countryside to the foreign Bransles and Corantos that had been introduced at Court in the 1660s and by the 1670s were being performed everywhere by the gentry.

The most popular of the seventeenth-century country dances was 'Roger de Coverley', which had originally been called 'The Haymakers' Jig', and was, in fact, one of the oldest of our English folk dances. Other country dances of the day with which the Winstanleys were doubtless familiar are 'The Shepherds' Dance', 'Sellenger's Round' and 'Gathering Peascods'.

The Christmas night dance was the merriest and most informal of the numerous dances held at Berries over the holidays. Consequently it was the one most conducive to romance. And during the years that William and Anne lived at the farm many declarations of love were probably made at this dance by eager swains. Both Will and his sister Anne were courting by the early 1680s, and the dark corners of the hall would have been ideal places in which to steal kisses and whisper confidences when the other members of the family were busily engaged in dancing and carousing near the fire.

Young Anne married Thomas Waite, a Saffron Walden malt-ster, in about 1682, and had one son, Thomas, of whom William Winstanley was very fond. Will married Frances Taylor, youngest daughter of John Taylor, Rector of Westmill, Hertfordshire, and sister to Elizabeth, wife of Henry Winstanley, the lighthouse builder, in 1684, and between 1687 and 1696 the couple produced four rumbustious little boys who were the delight of William's old age. He adored his beautiful daughter-in-law, too, whom he called his 'bonny Frank'. So all in all the marriages of his two eldest children brought him great joy. His youngest son, Thomas, never married, for he unfortunately died in 1696 at the age of eighteen.

The Winstanleys' Christmas night dances usually continued until dawn, and only ended, indeed, when the fiddlers became 'too weary to wield their bows longer'. They always managed to summon up enough strength to play one final feverishly fast jig, however, which left the dancers breathless but exhilarated. The guests then departed and the Winstanleys went to bed. And as William slowly climbed the stairs, his mind dwelling on all the happy merrymaking of the past twenty-four hours, he probably felt a little sad that his 'Golden Day of Days' was now over for another year, but took comfort from the thought that eleven more days of revelry still lay ahead.

BOXING DAY

EVERYONE got up very late at Berries on Boxing Day, and after a leisurely breakfast either went skating or sat by the fire in parlour or hall. During the Christmas holidays the womenfolk often sat sewing, reading and chatting in the parlour of a morning, while the men sat in the hall playing chess, draughts or backgammon, strumming musical instruments and singing snatches of song. Cider, perry and spiced ale 'flowed free' in the hall throughout the Christmas period, and there was always a cold pigeon pie, a bowl of frumenty and a plate of mince pies on the sideboard from which the guests could just help themselves. As the Winstanleys literally kept open house at Christmas, there was a perpetual coming and going of visitors over the Twelve Days, 'some rich; some poor', but all certain of receiving a warm welcome.

After William Winstanley had seen some of his guests off to Kitchen Pond and made the rest comfortable indoors, he himself went to the stables to perform the traditional Boxing Day bloodletting operation on his horses. Through a misunderstanding that occurred some time in the Middle Ages, the attributes of the ninth-century Swedish St Stephen, a great lover of horses, were grafted onto St Stephen, the first-century martyr, whose feast-day falls on 26th December. And although the martyr appears to have had absolutely no connection with horses whatsoever, he instead of the Swedish saint came to be regarded as their patron. It was believed, therefore, that if horses were ceremoniously bled on St Stephen's special day, this would ensure their health for the coming year. In the seventeenth century blood-letting was the panacea for all ills in both man and beast, and was often resorted to on a regular basis to preserve well-being. Winstanley was skilled in veterinary practice and would have known how to carry out this procedure quickly and humanely.

Horse in stable waiting to be let blood

Before the Reformation, Boxing Day had been the day on which the alms boxes in churches were opened and the money they contained shared out amongst the poor people of the parish. By the sixteenth century this custom had fallen into disuse, and apprentices, servants and errand boys went about asking for money from the wealthy on their own behalf at Christmas. This money was put into earthenware boxes with a narrow slit in the top, which were always broken open on Boxing Day. A few apprentices may still have carried round collecting boxes at Christmas in the late seventeenth century, but usually by that time they and their fellow servants were simply given small money presents by their masters on Boxing Day, and no longer had any need to beg.

William Winstanley, whose watchword at Christmas was 'liberality', would have been sure to give his own servants and farm labourers generous tips on Boxing Day, although he never mentions doing so. But the main beneficiaries of his largesse on this day were the poor of Quendon, to whom some time in the morning he and his wife and daughter distributed food, fuel and clothes. In most seventeenth-century yeoman families it was only the women and children who visited the poor, but William had such empathy with the destitute and felt such deep concern for their welfare that throughout the year he regularly called in to see them, and was especially anxious to alleviate their sufferings at Christmas.

The plight of the Quendon poor, as William describes it, was indeed desperate. Living in damp, draughty, tumbledown hovels with 'earthen' floors and 'leaking' roofs, they often 'had no money with which to buy Wood or Coals, scarce a stitch to their Backs, and little food to put in their Bellies.' He, the Lord of the Manor, and John Knight, who was Overseer of the Poor, did all they could to help them. But where infirmity, imbecility or drunkenness had brought families low it was sometimes difficult to ameliorate matters.

Winstanley possessed such powerful charisma that his presence in the midst of the sick and needy, laughing, chatting, telling stories, apparently did more to cheer them than the logs he brought, or the nourishing food or the cloaks and blankets, essential as these items were. He had inherited this knack of befriending the poor and putting them instantly at their ease from his mother, who had ministered to them with tireless devotion from her first arrival in Quendon. Her father, Samuel Leader, had instilled notions of compassion for the destitute and charity towards them into all his children. Elizabeth's twin brothers Samuel and William were perhaps the kindest benefactors that the poor of Saffron Walden have ever known. They gave endless sums of money to the Mayor and Corporation and to the churchwardens to help feed, clothe and house the needy, endowed places for them at the almshouse and left them substantial donations in their wills.

William Winstanley, who was comfortably off, but by no means rich, could not do so much for the poor in a material way. But from the 1660s until his death he wrote voluminously on their behalf; imploring everyone who had 'great store of pelf' and didn't know what to do with it to lay out some of their money in 'providing relief' for those who were 'sore oppressed by hunger and cold'; assuring them that 'another day' God would reward their generosity 'a thousand fold'. He realised, however, that in the nature of things, poverty would never be eradicated from the world, and thought that 'right to the end of Time some people will have too much, some too little, and none just enough'.

After delivering their Yuletide gifts to the Quendon poor, the Winstanleys returned to Berries for dinner, which on Boxing Day usually consisted of hot turkey pie, a variety of cold meats, plum puddings and mince pies. A light white wine would have gone well with this fairly simple fare. As Winstanley tells us that he loved 'the brisk, buxome, neat Canary' best of all white wines, this was probably the drink that accompanied the meal, although cider and beer would also have been available for those who preferred them.

To provide the children with some extra dessert and a little entertainment, at the end of the Boxing Day dinner William would fetch a basket containing apples, nuts, sweets and cakes, and placing 'the little boys and girls' in a row in front of him, proceeded to throw these delicacies 'all about the hall', while the youngsters raced madly up and down trying to catch them.

Weather permitting, after the midday meal on Boxing Day Winstanley always took the children for a nature ramble in Quendon Wood and the surrounding fields. He liked to enjoy their company as often as possible over the Christmas holidays, and as he had no special preparations to make for guests that evening, he could give the youngsters his full attention during the afternoon. A keen naturalist himself, he wanted to show his grandsons and great-nieces and nephews the myriad wonders of nature, and tried to make this annual walk as interesting as possible.

First he would take the children up to the small field behind Quendon Church, where there was a rabbit warren and they could 'watch the conies at their play'. Then he would point out the bank of long grass and brambles on the edge of Dovehouse Field where hares often lurked. And lastly they would go to Quendon Wood. William Winstanley had been familiar with this wood from his earliest childhood, and by the 1670s knew every tree, every clump of flowers, every

Rabbits at play

nesting site, set, earth and burrow within its bounds. To him the wood was a magical place where something exciting was sure to be glimpsed whenever he visited it, summer or winter alike, and he did his best to convey this enchantment to his young relatives.

In years when snow fell William would sometimes recite the following short poem about winter trees that he had composed in 1672, to amuse the children as they passed beneath the frozen branches:

Now trees their leafy hats do bare
To reverence Winter's silver hair.
And every hoary headed twig
Doth wear a snowy periwig.

He would then draw the children's attention to the beautiful shapes that the bare black and grey branches made against the sky, and teach them how to identify

Quendon Wood in winter

the 'majestic oaks', the 'tall Beech trees' and the coppiced 'hornebeams'. He showed the youngsters the hollow tree in which the 'Whooping owl' lived, the thicket where the magpies nested and the thick bush within which robins, wrens and oth-

Robin redbreast; from Thomas Bewick's History of British Birds, *published in 1797.*

er small birds sheltered from the cold. Robins were Winstanley's favourite birds, and he fed the tame robins that nested in the garden at Berries every day throughout the winter.

With his observant poet's eye William Winstanley spotted mosses and lichens, toadstools, catkins and the first green shoots of spring. All these things he would point out to the children, as well as the dreys of the red squirrels which then inhabited Quendon Wood, and the lairs of badgers and foxes. So during these Christmas rambles the youngsters must all have seen something to inspire them, and they probably learnt many facts about plants and animals that remained with them to the end of their days.

When they got back to Berries the children would be given a variety of hot caudles, possets and milk drinks, toast and honey and slices of cake or gingerbread. William calls this meal 'afternoon luncheon', but it was more usually known as 'beverages' or 'bevers', and while the men sometimes partook of it, it was mainly intended for women and children.

Between bevers and supper more Christmas games would be played. Hoodman Blind appears to have been the youngsters' favourite, but they also greatly enjoyed the thrilling version of indoor Hide-and-Seek that Winstanley had invented for them. In this game one set of players remained in a downstairs room which was called 'Home', and another set went off to hide in the dark bedrooms, store rooms and passages above. When they had all concealed themselves the leader would shout 'All-hid', and the seekers then began to look for them. If any of the hidden were able to outwit the seekers and reach 'Home' without being caught, they could go and hide again. But usually they were all discovered and triumphantly pounced upon, and it was then the seekers' turn to go and hide.

After supper on Boxing Day, William Winstanley would organise some quiet games for his adult guests 'by the fires-side'. Having stayed up so late the previous night everyone was a little tired, and there does not appear to have been any dancing that evening at Berries. Instead the company 'whiled away the hours until bed-time' very pleasantly by playing various card, dice and guessing games.

William's own favourite card game was 'One and Thirty', a type of cribbage for two, three or four players. Other card games that he tells us his family liked were 'Noddy, Ruff, Slam, Whisk, Uptails, All-Fours, Gleek, Best, Piquet and Primero'. Most of these games are mentioned in the first gaming manual to be published in England, John Cotton's *Compleat Gamester*, which came out in 1674. But Cotton's instructions are so obscure that apart from Whisk (Whist) and Piquet, which already had the same rules as the modern games, we cannot be sure how they were played.

From Cotton's explanations and from hints dropped by Winstanley himself we gather, however, that the family's best loved dice game, 'Hazard', was played with two dice by any number of people, and that the object was simply to guess one another's throws correctly. In 'Passage', a second dice game which was very popular with the Winstanleys, three dice were used,

Dice players, some wearing fancy dress, etched by Henry Winstanley in 1677.
By courtesy of the Ashmolean Museum, Oxford.

again any number could participate, and the aim was to shake the dice in turn until someone threw two doublets under ten, when they were out, or two over ten, when that person 'passed' and won the round.

Winstanley would not allow any betting or gambling to take place at Berries, so these games were never played for money. But occasionally, he informs us, small prizes such as 'a paper of pins', a 'Quill pen' or 'a little book of Rymes' would be given to the winners to add a fillip to the entertainment.

The 'Rymes' in these booklets may just have been ordinary poems. But the Winstanleys were so passionately fond of rhyming riddles that they are quite likely to have been riddles. Several collections of riddles were published in England in the sixteenth and seventeenth centuries, the most famous being Wynkyn de Worde's *Demandes Joyous* of 1511. And William Winstanley was always on the look-out for new riddles with which to puzzle his friends and relatives.

After repeating all the riddles by other people that he had managed to find during the previous twelve months, William would recite to the company the latest of the large number that over the years he himself devised. Some of these riddles appeared in successive editions of his *New Help to Discourse*, others in his almanacs. And three of them have stood the test of time and are still regularly included in modern anthologies and annuals.

The first is a witty description of teeth and tongue and runs as follows:

Four and twenty white Bulls
Sat upon a stall.
Forth came the Red-Bull,
And over-lickt them all.

The second describes a man with a thorn in his foot:

I went to the wood and I got it.
I sat me down and I sought it.
I kept it still against my will,
And so by force home I brought it.

The solution to the third is a robin redbreast, and the word 'Target' here is used in the old sense of a round shield or buckler, not a mark to shoot at. It goes:

I am called by the name of a man,
Yet am as little as a mouse.
When Winter comes I love to be
With my red Target near the house.

There was always much jollity and laughter at the Boxing Day riddle-telling sessions. And the Winstanleys and their guests so enjoyed guessing the answers that, sleepy as they were, they didn't want the fun to end. At last, however, the fire would begin to sink low, William would read out the final conundrum, and after it had been solved everyone retired to bed.

CHRISTMAS SPORTS & PASTIMES

THROUGHOUT the Twelve Days of Christmas the Winstanleys kept up a continual round of gaiety; not only feasting, dancing, singing and playing games in the traditional Yuletide manner, but also enjoying a whole range of other amusements unique to the family. When the weather was inclement they stayed indoors. But if it was fine they went out for much of the day for, like William, his brothers and sisters and their children were hardy, active individuals who loved fresh air and exercise.

In frosty years, as well as doing a lot of skating, the men and boys of the family had 'snowball fights' and built 'snow Castles with Towers and Pinnacles'. Whether these castles were small buildings like our modern sand castles, or larger, more ambitious structures is not known. Nor is it known whether snow castles were commonly made in the seventeenth century, or were a Winstanley innovation thought up by Henry the architect, who not only constructed lighthouses but several famous English country houses, too, including his own fine Baroque house at Littlebury.

When these pleasures of the snow and ice were denied to the Winstanleys through mild weather, they played football in Dovehouse Field or along Quendon Street. William tells us in his *Poor Robin's Perambulation* that the 'young men' of Quendon beat the youths 'from all the Towns about at Foot-ball play'. So Will and his companions probably practised regularly and would have been glad to take on a team of Winstanley cousins and uncles at Christmas, all of whom appear to have been very good at the game.

Quendon Street, along which the Winstanleys played football at Christmas.
Berries stood behind the belt of trees on the right.

A great variety of running, chasing and hiding games were played by both girls and boys in the garden, the rickyard and the shadowy barn at Berries. When these palled either William or Anne would take the children to visit some of the farm animals: a calf, perhaps, a new-born lamb or the horses and ponies.

We are not told whether the Winstanleys and their friends ever went out riding for exercise and enjoyment rather than merely to accomplish some journey, but as soon as they were old enough William certainly taught his youngest son and his grandsons to ride, and the long Christmas holidays would have been an ideal time for these lessons, which probably afforded the little boys keen delight.

Either on foot or on horseback William Winstanley always went to visit his three most powerful local patrons, Thomas Turner, Sir Thomas Middleton and James Howard, third Earl of Suffolk, some time over the Christmas period to wish them the compliments of the season and show his respect. He and Anne do not seem to have gone to see any of their other neighbouring friends and relatives at Yuletide – as host and hostess of a large house party, they felt they had to stay mainly at Berries to look after their guests – but all their acquaintances were warmly invited to come to them instead.

Thomas Turner of Quendon Hall was the first of his patrons that William would call upon. Ever since the Wilfords left the village, the successive owners of the hall had been on very cordial terms with the Winstanleys, and Thomas, who bought Quendon Hall in 1669, was no exception. As they sat over a glass of wine in the panelled parlour of the rambling, sixteenth-century hall, William and his host would have had much to discuss about village affairs, their crops, their animals and their respective families. By 1680 Thomas Turner would also describe to Winstanley his elaborate plans for pulling down old Quendon Hall and rebuilding it in a more modern style designed by Henry Winstanley. This work was begun just before Mr Turner's death in 1681, and was completed by his son John, who always remained as friendly towards the Winstanleys as his father had been.

By the 1680s Stansted Hall at Stansted Mountfitchet, four miles south of Quendon, had also been modernised, and now looked somewhat plain and gaunt, but the enthusiastic welcome that William Winstanley invariably received from the owner of the hall, Sir Thomas Middleton, more than made up for the building's forbidding appearance. Sir Thomas was the grandson of William's boyhood patron Timothy Middleton, and continued the family tradition of lending support to the author by encouraging him in all his literary projects and buying several copies of each of his works as soon as they were published. He too loved history and folklore, so he and William had much in common, and when the latter came to Stansted to pay his annual Christmas visit they probably spent many happy hours together discussing the latest historical controversies or the origins of Yuletide customs and traditions.

Winstanley's most illustrious Essex patron, James Howard, continued to live in his own set of lodgings at Audley End even after he had sold the house to Charles II in 1669, acting as

*Etching of Audley End
made by Henry Winstanley in 1703.*

Royal Housekeeper there until his death in 1688. William, who considered Jacobean Audley End with its towers and turrets, courtyards and colonnades, to be one of the finest houses in the whole of Europe and called it 'a most gallant, uniform Building', was greatly relieved that the Earl of Suffolk had not been asked to move, for he thoroughly enjoyed riding over to the mansion at Christmas time to see the Howards. When he arrived he always found much feasting and jollification going on in the earl's hall, for James Howard kept as merry a Yule as Winstanley himself, and during the holidays hired musicians, mummers and puppeteers to entertain his guests.

In the 1670s the Earl of Suffolk still often went to Court and was one of Charles II's closest friends. His successful defence of Landguard Fort off Harwich during the Dutch War of 1667, when he and his handful of retainers were heavily outnumbered by the marauders, had won him the reputation of being the bravest man in England, and he was also universally respected for his honesty and integrity. By the early 1680s, however, he had become gout-ridden and infirm and rarely left Audley End.

William Winstanley continued to venerate the earl as a heroic figure until the last, however. Not only had he defended his country in her hour of need as valiantly as the chivalrous knights of old, whom William regarded as the ideal of English manhood, but from 1640 onwards he had befriended the entire Winstanley family and done his utmost to further both William's career and that of his nephew Henry. At all times, therefore, he and his wife showed James Howard every attention in their power. At Christmas, in addition to a present from himself, William doubtless took the earl a box of marchpane or some other culinary delicacy from Anne as a token of her esteem.

On cold, wet, stormy days over Christmas, when it was impossible to get out, William Winstanley provided various amusements for his guests indoors. All the Winstanleys loved dressing up and play-acting, so sometimes he would suggest that the whole family should work together to produce a simple play. We are not told the subject matter of any of these plays, which appear to have been written by William and Henry in collaboration. But when Henry opened his 'Mathematicall Water Theatre' in Piccadilly in

1696, the plots he used for the tableaux that he staged there were all taken either from classical mythology or from romance literature, and dealt with such themes as the exploits and amorous adventures of gods and goddesses or the attempts of knights and squires to rescue princesses from dragons, giants and magicians. Identical themes were also employed by William in his poetry and novels. So it seems likely that the Christmas plays at Berries were based on this type of material, which could easily have been turned into comical, pantomime-style farces, with singing, dancing and even perhaps one or two of the transformation scenes for which Henry Winstanley's theatre was renowned.

Henry knew how to create wonderfully realistic dragons out of 'painted canvas, pasteboard and dry, light wood', which could be made to flap their wings and belch smoke out of their mouths in a very satisfactory manner. The children would have enjoyed constructing one of these monsters under his direction. They would doubtless also have liked to make and operate a giant similar to the theatrical 'mock Gyant' that William Winstanley describes in *Sir Billy of Billericay*, which was 'fashioned' by stretching canvas over a wooden frame on wheels. This giant was 'armed with a Pole-Axe', and William informs us that a person inside the frame 'could make him to move his weapon, shake his head and perform any other Action of his Body as if he were alive; then for speech, a hollow Trunk through his head into his Mouth delivered what they would speak by him.'

Scenery may have been painted for the Winstanleys' Christmas plays by Henry and the children, and costumes sewn by the

Christmas revels at Haddon Hall, Derbyshire,
with dragons and mock giants very like
those the Winstanleys created at Berries.

women of the family. The plays were probably either put on in the hall at Berries or in the barn outside. But whether the public at large was admitted to see them or they were strictly private affairs is not known.

Both William Winstanley and his nephew Henry believed that the artistic abilities inherent in all children should be encouraged as much as possible. And in the years when no Christmas play was acted they would provide the youngsters with pencils and water colours and teach them the rudiments of drawing and painting. William was the first man in England, and probably in the whole of Europe, to recognise the potential of abstract art, and often tells his readers that random shapes and geometric designs are 'handsom things to look upon' and should be better appreciated. So if his small grandsons produced only squiggles and blobs in their early attempts at painting, they would have gained his sympathetic understanding if no one else's.

To amuse the children at Yuletide and give them an incentive to practise their writing, William would also show them how to make a most effective invisible ink out of 'the juice of a Limon'. First the lemon juice would be squeezed out onto a plate, and then 'with a clean Pen' a 'secret message' would be written in juice on a sheet of paper. As soon as the words of the message were dry they disappeared and could not be read by the recipient of the note until he held the paper 'close to the Fire', when, as if by magic, dark brown lettering began to form.

After spending a quiet morning or afternoon painting and writing, the children would probably have welcomed the chance to participate in more active sports, and two such games that Winstanley tells us were played indoors at Berries during the Christmas holidays were 'Leaping over Stooles' and 'Bobbing for Apples'. In the stool game boys first had to jump over one stool, then two stools placed together, then three, without touching any of them with their hands, feet or legs. The apple game was played by suspending a large pippin on a string high above the youngsters' heads, when they took it in turns to jump up and see who would be the first to take a bite out of the fruit.

These games were too boisterous for the very young children to play, and what they liked best was to sit on William's knee or at his feet or clustered round his chair while he told them stories by the parlour fire. For his son Tom, his grandsons Thomas, Tom, William, Harry and John and his favourite great-niece Fanny, daughter of Charles Winstanley, William in fact kept a special stock of entrancing Christmas legends, fairy stories and fantasy tales that he recounted to nobody else. And he much enjoyed having the little ones to himself now and then at Yuletide so as to be able to talk to them and really get to know them.

In order to make Christmas meaningful to the toddlers and convey to them something of the season's essential magic, William would explain the Nativity story in simple terms and also tell them a few of the legends that surround the festival. The Christmas legend that he liked best was the tale of the 'miraculous Glastonbury hawthorn' that is supposed suddenly to have sprouted and blossomed when Joseph of Arimathea thrust his staff into the ground at Weary-all Hill in Glastonbury, and ever afterwards burst into bloom on Christmas Eve. But he would also narrate to the children the story of how at exactly midnight on Christmas Eve the cattle in their byres and the horses in their stables were believed to turn to the east and kneel down to worship the newly born Christ Child, just as the ox and the ass had honoured Him on that first Christmas Night long ago.

The fairy tales that Winstanley told the youngsters were the traditional seventeenth-century fairy stories that described how by day the 'Fairy Elves' spent most of their time 'dancing and sporting themselves' in the woods. Under cover of darkness, however, they would creep into farms and cottages and either 'rob the Dairy' or 'help the Churning' as the mood took them. If the house visited was

Woodcut of c. 1670, showing fairies dancing in a ring.

neat and tidy the fairies might drop a sixpence into the maid's shoe as a reward for cleanliness. But if it was dirty they would pinch the 'slatternly Wench' in her sleep.

All these varied tales held the youngsters spellbound, and as soon as one was finished they clamoured eagerly for more. The adults of the family were as captivated by William Winstanley's stories as the children. And it seems that almost every night throughout the Christmas holidays he would tell them a few of his 'merry tales'. Some of these narratives were folk tales and adventure stories of the type that he recounted on Christmas Eve. But others were the sort of joke story that he published in his almanacs and in his book *Poor Robin's Jests, or the Compleat Jester*. This work was reprinted seventeen times between 1667 and 1760, and remained the most popular joke book in England until it was partially eclipsed in 1739 by *Joe Miller's Jests*, the most famous joke collection ever published in this country.

Several of the jokes in the Joe Miller anthology appear to have been taken from Winstanley's book, and he in turn probably obtained many of his jests from the large number of joke books that had been in circulation since 1600. Very few of these seventeenth-century jokes seem funny to us now, for fashions in humour change almost as rapidly as fashions in clothes and are as little understood by succeeding generations, but the following two jokes from *Poor Robin's Jests* were perennial favourites right down to the 1890s, and may still perhaps raise a smile today.

The first of these joke stories concerns a lady who went to dine with friends, and during the course of the evening was questioned about her age, 'which she affirmed to be but Forty'. Her friends still doubting, she finally called out to one of the gentlemen in the company, 'Cousin, do you believe I am in the right when I say I am but Forty?'

'I ought not to dispute you, Madam', reply'd he, 'for I have heard you say so these ten Years.'

The second story refers to 'a gentleman not quite so wise as Solomon', who was eating a large piece of Cheshire cheese one night at a tavern. When he had finished the cheese, which was 'pretty full of Maggots', he said to his companions, 'Now have I done as much as Sampson, for I have destroyed my thousands and my ten thousands.'

'Ah, Sir, so you have', answered a wag, 'and with the same weapon, too – the jawbone of an ass.'

Winstanley appears to have been particularly fond of simpleton jests, a great many of which were published in his newspaper and almanacs as well as in his joke book. The wittiest of these jests are the series of tales about the 'Hobbodeboobies' of northwest Essex that began to appear in his *Poor Robin's Almanacks* from 1690 onwards. To give the jokes point and immediacy William pretended that they had been perpetrated by simpletons living in his vicinity, but they must actually have been his own inventions.

In his almanac for 1693, for example, William tells us about poor, dim-witted 'Frank P. of Walden', who 'with much earnestness desired to know which day of the week Shrove Tuesday was on'. In 1694 he describes the antics of the 'crazy Miller of Quendon', who one day in the previous year had 'rid upon his mare to enquire of his neighbours if they could tell any tidings of her'. And in the almanac for 1697 we are presented with the sorry tale of 'the old Sadler of Wal... who went fourteen miles for a Licence to marry a Widow, but when he came there he had forgot her name'.

Perhaps the best of these Hobbodebooby jokes, however, is the one concerning 'A.N. of Newport', who, in a fit of temper in 1698, shouted out to his father, 'Don't you know what injury you have done me? Why, had you not been born, I should have inherited all my Grandfather's wealth.'

NEW YEAR

A GRAND, festive supper, to which all William Winstanley's friends and relatives were invited, always took place at Berries on New Year's Eve. He believed that the only fitting way to 'conclude the good old year' was to 'let Gates and doors wide open be' and offer 'lavish hospitality' to everyone who came through them.

The bill of fare on this occasion consisted of 'Joints of Beef, Pork and Mutton', together with a variety of game such as 'Pheasants, Partridges, Mallard, Teal, Roasted Pidgeons and Hares and Venison Pasties'. These viands were accompanied by appropriate gravies and sauces, some carrots, onions, parsnips and potatoes and a great many white Christmas loaves, which William tells us on this special night 'ran up and down the table like bowls in an alley'.

Tall, cylindrical 'flaggons' of 'Sack, Claret, Canary, Malago and Musquadine' also passed briskly round the table, as did jugs of ale, cider and perry. Mince pies, fruit tarts and plum puddings formed the dessert. And when this was over the company seated themselves round the hall fire, where a huge bowl of lambswool

Flagons and tankards
like those the Winstanleys used at New Year
from Randolph Caldicottt's Old Christmas,
1875.

reposed on the hob and on either side of the hearth stood small side tables laden with dishes of cakes and sweetmeats, to which the guests were cordially invited to help themselves.

In the seventeenth century many families played divination games with chestnuts, apples and candles on New Year's Eve. But as Winstanley deeply distrusted all forms of fortune-telling and prediction, considering that it was 'dangerous to pry into forbid secrets too nigh', it seems unlikely that such games would have been played at Berries. In those days New Year's Eve was also the time when ghost stories were generally told, for it was believed that on this magical night, poised precariously between past and future, the barriers separating this world and the next were down and spirits walked abroad. William had no objection to ghost stories, of which, indeed, he was an avid collector, and when everyone had been well supplied with sweets, lambswool and tobacco after supper on New Year's Eve, it was his invariable custom to entertain his guests with a selection of these eerie tales.

Throughout his life Winstanley remained basically sceptical about supernatural occurrences. It is to be presumed, therefore, that he did not believe in ghosts any more than he believed in fairies, but stories about 'unearthly beings' intrigued him and appealed strongly to his poetic imagination.

William Winstanley's favourite ghost stories concerned the *ignis fatuus* or 'Will with the Wisp' as he called it, which haunted church-yards, moorlands and marshy places in many parts of England in the seventeenth century. This weird, uncanny light, which appeared like either a ball of fire or a candle flame, some-times burnt steadily in one area and at other times suddenly shot up in the air or darted hither

Engraving of a Will-o'-the-Wisp executed by Otto Speckter in 1887.

and thither a few feet above the ground. Essex folk thought that the light must belong to some mischievous spirit, bogey or hobgoblin who delighted in teasing travellers and leading them astray. Over the years William had heard several accounts of benighted Essex pedlars, carters and farm labourers who had been 'allured to death and misadventure' by the dancing, flickering flames. As the men advanced towards the lights, believing them to be lanterns or lighted windows, they had lost their way 'or fallen headlong into Ditches or Ponds'. William and his kith and kin tried to puzzle out what on earth the *ignis fatuus* could be, but had to conclude in the end that the mystery was insoluble.

Winstanley's great friends the Cooks, who kept the Crown Inn at 'Hockrell' in Bishop's Stortford, Hertfordshire, just over the Essex border from Quendon, where both Charles II and William III regularly dined on their way to attend the races at Newmarket, had told him about the 'White Lady' who haunted the churchyard of St Michael's Church in Stortford and scared late passers-by into fits. He related this story to his guests on New Year's Eve. He also gave an account of the ghostly footsteps, cries and groans that had often been heard in various parts of the Tower of London by his friend Sir John Robinson, Lieutenant of the Tower.

From ghost stories William would move on to tales of witches and wizards, who at that time were also supposed to be out and about on New Year's Eve. He appears to have been particularly fascinated by the biblical account of the Witch of Endor, and by the prophecies of the famous Yorkshire witch, Mother Shipton. Winstanley also knew the case histories of all the women in-

Seventeenth-century woodcut of flying witches.

volved in the three sixteenth-century Chelmsford witch trials.

A great many white wizards, known as Cunning Men, lived in Essex in the seventeenth century. Some of these wizards charmed away warts and healed the sick and would accept no payment from their patients. Others were charlatans who pretended to be able to read the future, brew up love potions or locate missing articles and charged exorbitant fees for their services. In 1651 William's brother James had had a bizarre encounter with one of the latter type of wizard, the Cunning Man of Berden, details of which he might sometimes be prevailed upon to narrate to the company at Christmas time, although he was rather ashamed of the story.

The encounter came about because on 26th March 1651 Elizabeth Winstanley's draper's shop had been broken into in the night, and she had lost '29 yards of greene say worth £4 and £4 in ready money'. James, who was still living at Berries at this time and was probably about eighteen, told his friend Edward Stephens about the robbery and Stephens suggested that the two of them should go and ask the Berden wizard, William Hills, how to catch the thief, for he apparently specialised in 'the discovery and finding out of stolen goods'. The boys went over to Berden, three miles to the west of Quendon, therefore, told Hills all about the robbery and begged him to assist Elizabeth in recovering her possessions. The wizard said that he would 'doe them the best helpe he could', drew up an elaborate astrological figure and then told the youngsters a long rigmarole about who the thieves were and where to look for the missing goods.

Acting on William Hills' advice the boys returned to Quendon, and, accompanied by the village constable, Thomas Law, 'searched divers howses' in Quendon and Rickling but found nothing. When Elizabeth learnt that James had consulted 'an evil Cunning Man' about her goods and had given him money she was horrified and immediately had Hills brought before her friend Timothy Middleton of Stansted Hall, who was the nearest JP. Here she accused the wizard of 'using divers deceitful and unlawful arts to abuse and cozen the good people of this Commonwealth'. And although William Hills defended himself by saying that he had learnt 'the Art of Astrology' from the famous astrologer William Lilly in London, and only took such reward for practising this art 'as people themselves would give', he was sternly forbidden ever to make use of astrology again and bound over to keep the peace. Mrs Winstanley's goods were never recovered, but had probably been stolen by a passing tramp rather than a fellow villager.

After the story-telling on New Year's Eve there was always dancing. And while the company 'footed it merrily' a cold buffet of oysters, ham, chicken, turkey and mince pies would be laid out by the servants on the hall table. This second supper was eaten at about midnight, and when 'the New Year's joyous Chimes' began to sound from Quendon Church, everyone raised their glasses to pledge the new-born year. Kisses and good wishes were then exchanged. Afterwards family and guests all joined in singing the traditional New Year carol, 'The Old Year Now Away is Fled', that was sung to the tune of 'Greensleeves' in almost every home in the land from 1642 to 1700. The first four verses run as follows:

The old year now away is fled,
The new year it is entered,
Then let us now our sins down tread
And joyfully all appear.
Let's merry be this holiday,
And let us now both sport and play,
Hang sorrow, let's cast care away:
God send you a happy New Year!

And now with New-Year's gifts each friend,
Unto each other they do send;

God grant we may all our lives amend,
And that the truth may appear.
Now like the snake cast off your skin
Of evil thoughts and wicked sin,
And to amend this New Year begin,
God send us a merry New Year!

And now let all the company,
In friendly manner all agree,
For we are here welcome, all may see;
Unto this jolly good cheer.
I thank my master and my dame,
The which are founders of the same;
To eat, to drink is now no shame:
God send us a merry New Year!

Come lads and lasses every one,
Jack, Tom, Dick, Bessy, Mary and Joan,
Let's cut the meat up unto the bone,
For welcome you need not fear;
And here for good liquor you shall not lack,
It will whet my brains and strengthen my back,
This jolly good cheer it must go to wrack:
God send us a merry New Year!

Soon after the carol singing the party broke up and the
Winstanleys went to bed. Here the adults of the family no doubt
reposed soundly, but William tells us that the children 'hardly

slept a Wink' so excited were they by the prospect of all the 'fine New-Year Gifts' they expected to receive on the morrow.

The presents that the Winstanleys gave to one another were handed round at the breakfast table on New Year's Day. And this private family gift distribution was always a very merry occasion. For William says that as well as exchanging mundane presents such as 'clothes and Household Stuffe', the grown-ups went to great lengths every Christmas to procure for each other a few 'rarities' that would surprise and delight the recipient. We are not told what any of these unusual gifts were but in that inventive and imaginative family they probably ranged from original gadgets such as small clocks, musical boxes and automata created by Henry Winstanley to some of the standard 'rarities' that were so much prized by virtuosos in that age – miniature Bibles and poetry books, curious shells, gemstones, coins and medals, flies trapped in lumps of amber, sharks' teeth or cups allegedly made from unicorn horns.

Presents that had been made by the giver were always highly valued in the seventeenth century, and many other members of the Winstanley clan must have distributed home-made gifts at New Year as well as Henry. William doubtless presented the womenfolk with bottles of the perfumes that he made at Berries, and gave the men and boys some of the quill pens that he was so

Overleaf: An example of one of the 'rarities' that Henry Winstanley gave his relatives at New Year in 1678: copies of his newly invented 24-year calendar. By courtesy of Worcester College, Oxford.

good at cutting. Anne probably gave boxes of sweets, pots of jam and slabs of her dark, spicy gingerbread. And William's sisters Mary and Anne, being accomplished needlewomen like their mother, may have sewn dresses, cushion covers, napkins and tablecloths for the family.

Little girls were usually set to work hemming handkerchiefs or embroidering slippers and purses for their friends and relatives at Christmas in the seventeenth century, while the boys were encouraged to make wooden stools, boxes and bookcases. So the Winstanley children probably produced some of these handi-crafts, and also perhaps a few letters in invisible ink and a sheaf of abstract drawings to amuse William.

From their grandparents, uncles and aunts the Winstanley youngsters appear to have received a positive avalanche of gifts in return. William specifically mentions buying 'Drums, Trumpets and Books' for his children and grandsons. As he is known to have purchased board games, packs of cards, balls and skittles for the family in general, it is reasonable to assume that quite a few of these items, too, were destined for the small fry. Anne gave children boxes of 'Sugar Candy'. And Henry, who was very fond of youngsters but never had any of his own, made his nephews and nieces miniature windmills, kites, musical boxes and clockwork toys. All the Winstanleys doted on their offspring, so the chil-dren would have been sure to obtain a great many presents from their parents as well.

In addition to gifts from their family, William and Anne re-ceived a constant stream of presents from friends, patrons and

Woodcut of the 1690s,
showing a post boy delivering Christmas mail

well-wishers throughout New Year's Day. These generally took the form of turkeys, geese, capons, game birds, haunches of venison, barrels of oysters and bottles of wine, although occasionally a pewter flagon or tankard or a piece of plate might be sent. The gifts came from all over England and were brought either by carrier or by special messenger. William for his part sent food and drink, books and curios to all the distant friends and patrons he wished to remember. Henry, the lighthouse builder, is also known to have been showered with New Year gifts, and while most of these probably went to his house at Littlebury, a few may have been delivered to Berries.

All the comestibles received must have been very useful in helping to feed William's numerous guests over the holiday period, and some of them doubtless appeared on the New Year dinner table. Only members of the family were invited to dine at Berries on New Year's Day, so the midday meal was a pleasant, intimate, fairly simple affair, consisting of 'Calve's Head and Bacon', the traditional English New Year dish at that time, mince pies, plum puddings and whatever other viands Anne had seen fit to add from the vast assortment of delicacies that had been sent to the family.

After dinner the children played with their new toys in the hall; tooted their trumpets, beat their drums, and ate their way through quantities of sweets, fruit, nuts and cakes. Their elders spent the afternoon and evening by the parlour fire, reminiscing about the year that had gone and discussing plans for the year ahead. The Winstanleys liked to revive only agreeable memories and look forward confidently to future joys, for they strongly believed in the importance of positive thinking, and considered that 'to be Content is worth more than any Gold'. These sound doctrines stood the family in good stead, for by and large all the Essex Winstanleys led happy lives and managed to accomplish the fulfilment of their dreams.

TWELFTH NIGHT

IN THE SEVENTEENTH CENTURY Twelfth Night (6th January), the Feast of the Epiphany, was regarded as the greatest 'High-day' of the year after Christmas Day, and most families celebrated the occasion with a series of festivities which were designed both to honour the Three Kings and to end the Christmas season with appropriate éclat. Certainly at Berries 'Frolicsome revelry' was kept up from morning to night at Epiphany, and it would seem that William Winstanley was particularly fond of this festival, which he mentions repeatedly in his writings.

In his *Pathway to Knowledge*, for example, William describes Epiphany as 'a Feast Solemnised in memory of Christ's Manifestation to the Gentiles by a miraculous blazing-star, by virtue whereof three kings were conducted to adore him in the Manger, where they presented him on this day with Gold, Myrrh and Frankincense, in testimony of his Royalty, Humanity and Divinity'. And it was mainly, perhaps, on account of the 'miraculous blazing-star' that Winstanley was so attracted to the Epiphany story. To him stars were the most magical, the most poetic, the most sublime objects in the whole of creation, and he

The Three Kings offering their gifts to the Christ Child

never tired of praising their 'Lustrous Beauty'.

William's nephew Henry shared his love of stars, and on fine summer evenings the two men often climbed up to the lantern on the roof of Henry's house in Littlebury to study these luminaries through a telescope. William conjectured that the 'Holy star' which guided the Wise Men to Bethlehem must have been much larger and brighter than any of the stars that he and Henry had ever seen, however, and to the end of his life it continued to exert a powerful fascination over him.

The best way to show his reverence for this wondrous star, the Christ Child and the Three Kings was, William thought, to offer his guests even more lavish hospitality on Twelfth Night than he normally did at Christmas time. So he always planned a succession of treats for that day, which invariably culminated at night in a special banquet and party.

First came a substantial dinner at midday, attended by the whole Essex Winstanley clan, all the Winstanleys' friends in the vicinity and several poor Quendon families. Every table, chair, bench and stool at Berries, in Thomas Winstanley's cottage and in the houses of their near neighbours must have been pressed into service in order to seat the multitude of guests who were invited to this Twelfth Night dinner, and when everyone had taken their places the hall was probably rather crowded. But this would not have worried William, who believed that over the entire Christmas period

Yet more the merrier is the best,
As well of dishes as of guests.

The dishes provided at this meal mainly consisted of the old, traditional English Christmas fare – 'Roast Beef, Boiled Beef and Powdered Beef' – vast joints of which were borne to table on pewter chargers and platters, accompanied by 'good, strong Mustard' and potato pies. There were also 'Collars of Brawn, pigeon pies, sausages and venison Pasties'. For dessert the company enjoyed fruit tarts, bowls of fruit and nuts and the last mince pies and plum puddings of the holiday, served with clotted cream. William Winstanley's strongest beer and most full-bodied claret was drunk with the first course; his finest canary with the dessert, and after the meal his guests were offered the choice of lambswool or brandy.

When the visitors were all clustered round the fire and the superfluous tables and chairs had been removed, there was quite a large space left at one end of the hall for playing Christmas games. At Berries the afternoon of Twelfth Night appears to have been entirely devoted to these 'merry sports and gambols', in which not only the children but also several adults participated.

All the popular seventeenth-century indoor Christmas games such as Hoodman Blind, Hot Cockles and Hunt the Slipper were played, as well as 'Nine Pins or Skittles', which William tells us was one of the Winstanleys' favourite sports. Two other games that many seventeenth-century families played at this season were a forerunner of the modern Oranges and Lemons and a singing game where children danced round in a circle, called Here We Go Round the Bramble Bush. Although William does not mention either of these popular games, it is probable that some of his friends or relatives would have known them and introduced them at Berries.

After these frolics, a few carols were sung; a few stories told. The children were then provided with sweets, cakes and drinks for their afternoon bevers. By the time they had finished this snack it would be growing dark outside and the moment had come to 'Wassail the Fruit-trees.'

The custom of wassailing orchard trees on Twelfth Night has always mainly belonged to the cider-producing areas of the West Country, and was not usually practised in Essex in the seventeenth century. But William Winstanley considered it to be such a pleasant old custom that when he inherited Berries in 1670 he decided to adopt it for the amusement of his family and friends. Originally the wassailing ritual had been conducted as a serious magical rite intended to protect the fruit trees from evil spirits and make them bear bumper crops, but by the seventeenth century the ritual was simply carried out to bring luck to the trees and provide an enjoyable outing for the participants. Certainly the wassailing that took place in the orchard at Berries on Twelfth Night every year 'occasioned Great mirth.'

Well wrapped up in their cloaks, greatcoats, waxed boots and gloves the party set out soon after dark carrying lanterns, drums, tin trumpets, assorted fireworks and William's 'old Fowling-piece', and made their way to the orchard behind the house. Here they gathered round the tallest apple tree (which symbolically represented all the trees), and after William had poured the contents of a bowl of cider over the roots as a libation, the tree was gaily

Woodcut of c. 1690,
showing boys picking 'hats and sacks full' of apples

serenaded. We are not told which of the numerous seventeenth-century wassail songs the Winstanleys sang, but one of the most popular of these songs was the following ditty:

Here stands a good apple tree;
Stand fast at root,
Bear well at top;
Every little twig
Bear an apple big;
Every little bough
Bear apples enow;
Hats full! Caps full!
Three-score sacks full!
Holla, boys, Holla!

At the close of the song all the children shouted, cheered, beat their drums and blew their trumpets 'as loud as may be', the men let off 'squibs and crackers' and William fired his gun through the topmost branches of the apple tree. In pagan times this sort of cacophony had been created to frighten off any spectres or boggarts that might be lurking in the orchard. But the Winstanleys just regarded it all as a bit of 'harmless sport' to entertain the children, who must, indeed, have found the wassailing a very exciting experience.

After this ritual was concluded several of the guests took their departure. Some had Twelfth Night parties of their own to organise. Others had long distances to travel and wished to reach home before it grew too late. Most of the Winstanleys stayed on for the banquet and rollicking evening party at Berries, however. And sometimes one or two of William's literary friends from London, such as John Aubrey or George Etherege, came to the party and spent the night at the farm. The most frequent of these Twelfth Night guests appears to have been Sir Roger L'Estrange, the staunchly Royalist publisher of the *London Gazette* and the *Observator*, translator of *Aesop's Fables* and the official Press Censor. Charming, witty, urbane and very fond of music, singing and dancing, Sir Roger was an ideal guest, and in the years when he was present doubtless helped to make the Winstanleys' Twelfth Night festivities go with a swing.

Before Anne went up to dress for the party, she helped her cook to prepare a few of the somewhat complex supper dishes. Meanwhile Winstanley and his manservant consulted together about the various wines that would be required in the course of the evening. William then supervised the laying of the long dining table in the hall and, when the pewter, silver and napery had been arranged to his satisfaction, he fetched a box of the best wax candles with which to illuminate the festive board. All the feasts that Winstanley held at Christmas were basically merry, informal affairs, but the Twelfth Night supper with its spectacular array of sumptuous dishes was perhaps slightly less informal than the other meals. William wanted to be sure that on this grand occasion the table itself matched the splendour of the comestibles.

A huge bowl of especially rich, creamy frumenty always formed the first course of the Twelfth Night banquet at Berries. The Winstanley family as a whole had a particular weakness for cream, and on this last evening of the Christmas holidays Anne indulged them in it to the full.

The meat course then arrived in all its glory, with a 'Roasted Swan' as centre-piece and a turkey, a goose and several ducks and capons surrounding it like satellites. Swan was often eaten at Christmas in the seventeenth century and was regarded as a choice delicacy. The Winstanleys' Twelfth Night swans were probably sent to them as an

Swan,
from Thomas Bewick's
History of British Birds, *1797*

annual gift by one of William's friends or patrons, but at that time swans could also be purchased from poulterers.

Hannah Woolley does not give any directions for roasting a swan in her *Queene-Like Closet*, although she includes a recipe for 'Swan Pie', in which she says that the flesh of this bird should always be seasoned 'very well with Pepper, Salt and Ginger' and thoroughly larded before cooking. So the Winstanleys' swan, roasted on a spit before the kitchen fire, may have been prepared in this way. Mrs Woolley advises her readers to garnish the dish on which the Swan pie is served with bay leaves and lemon peel, and these decorations may also have been traditional with roast swan.

In whatever manner the Twelfth Night swan was brought to table at Berries, however, we may be sure that it presented a magnificent appearance and was greatly relished by all the guests. It is known that in the seventeenth century, roast swan was always accompanied by a very rich sauce. Hannah Woolley's 'Sauce for all Fowles' would certainly meet this criterion, being composed of 'Claret Wine, Vinegar, Anchovies, Oisters, Nutmeg, Shelots, Gravie of Mutton or Beef, Sweet Butter, Juice of a Limon and a little Salt'. This may well have been the sauce used at Berries, therefore.

For dessert Anne Winstanley and her cook had prepared a mouth-watering selection of creamy dishes to regale the company – trifles, jellies, cheesecakes, syllabubs and, creamiest of all, 'a caudle Sack posset', William's favourite pudding, which was a sort of thick, alcoholic custard containing sack, sugar, eggs, spices and many pints of cream. As the Essex Winstanleys all appear to have been blessed with sound digestions, they were able to do full justice to these delectable concoctions and then somehow still find room for a piece of the resplendent Twelfth cake that was ceremoniously borne into the hall along with the silver wassail bowl as soon as dessert was over.

In the seventeenth century the Twelfth cakes were a vital part of the festive proceedings that took place in most homes on the evening of Twelfth Night. Winstanley informs us that they contained 'the Bean and the Pea by which the King and Queen are chosen', and it was this monarch and his consort who presided over the after-supper revels, rewarding the winners of the various

Woodcut depicting a Twelfth-Night party c. 1800.
On the table is the sort of Twelfth cake the Winstanleys enjoyed.

games played, exacting forfeits from the losers and frequently is-
suing nonsensical orders which their subjects had promptly to
obey.

By tradition Twelfth cakes were supposed to be heavily iced
and lavishly adorned with painted sugar roses, crowns, stars,
castles, knights, dragons and little figures of the Three Kings, so
they were almost invariably bought from a pastry cook and not
made at home. William and Anne followed this custom, and the
method they used for cutting the cake and selecting the Twelfth

Night King and Queen remained the normal one in England until the beginning of the eighteenth century when the King and Queen were chosen by means of cards placed in a hat and not by the bean and pea in the cake.

First all the Winstanleys admired the Twelfth cake, pointing out its myriad beauties and exclaiming over them. Then William cut the glorious confection into exactly as many slices as there were people at the table, and each person took a piece. If a man found the bean in his portion, he became King, but if a woman found it she had the right to choose a King. The woman who discovered the pea in her slice of cake was crowned Queen, but if a man found the pea he could name a Queen.

At Berries the wassail bowl, which on this occasion was filled with sweet white wine instead of lambswool, circulated round the board while the Twelfth cake was being eaten. Everyone drank toasts to each other, wishing the person pledged health and prosperity in the year ahead.

In most families the Twelfth Night King and Queen were crowned with gilt paper crowns and robed in finery before they began their brief reign. As the Winstanleys were so fond of dressing up, it seems likely that this is what happened in the hall at Berries as soon as the supper things had been cleared away. Which Twelfth Night games were then played is not known. All William tells us is that they were 'very jolly'. The usual sports indulged in on this night in the seventeenth century, however, ranged from boisterous games such as mock battles and tugs of war to quieter pastimes like charades, crambo, kissing games, guessing games and competitions to see who could recite the longest poem or the cleverest riddle. And these must have been the sort of games that the Winstanleys and their friends enjoyed on Twelfth Night.

At about eleven o'clock the games at Berries came to an end, and William and Anne, assisted by their children and servants, began to take down all the Christmas greenery in the house. Traditionally this had to be burnt before midnight struck on Twelfth Night or bad luck would follow. William describes how the sprigs of holly, ivy, bay and rosemary 'sputtered and burst into Flame' when they were thrown onto the fire. As he watched the twigs burn he may have recited to the company Robert Herrick's famous poem 'Ceremony', about taking down the Christmas decorations, which he much admired. It runs as follows:

> Down with the Rosemary, and so
> Down with the Bais and mistletoe;
> Down with the Holly, Ivie, all
> Wherewith ye drest the Christmas Hall:
> That so the superstitious find
> No one least Branch there left behind:
> For look, how many leaves there be
> Neglected there (maids trust to me)
> So many goblins you shall see.

When every scrap of greenery had been reduced to ashes, it would be time to partake of the cold collation that had been set out on the hall table. This was probably very similar to the late supper provided on New Year's Eve. At its conclusion the Twelfth Night King, as was customary, would have made a speech thanking William and Anne for their generous hospitality and asking the company to show their appreciation of their host and hostess by giving them a hearty round of applause.

In the background the pipers and fiddlers now began to tune their instruments for the last dance of the holiday. Soon the gentlemen were choosing partners for 'Gathering Peascods' or 'Roger de Coverley'. The musicians then struck up 'a blithesome air', and away the couples went, advancing, retreating, bowing, curtsying and dancing up and down the sets with great verve and spirit. As the night wore on the music grew ever faster and faster; the couples leapt ever higher and higher, until finally the exhausted musicians could play no more and reluctantly brought the dance to a close.

As the notes of the last hectic jig died away, Christmas came to an end at Berries. But glorious memories of all the merry junketings that had taken place at the farm over the Yuletide period remained with the Winstanleys and their friends throughout the rest of the year; gladdening their hearts and sustaining them in moments of difficulty. They were further sustained by the thought that the Christmas season would, in fact, very soon return, when they would all be gathered together once more beneath William's hospitable roof, and the delightful round of feasting, dancing and merrymaking would start all over again.

APPENDIX

RECIPES
FOR SOME OF
THE CHRISTMAS FARE
ENJOYED BY WILLIAM WINSTANLEY
AND HIS FAMILY

TAKEN FROM
HANNAH WOOLLEY'S
QUEENE-LIKE CLOSET

TO MAKE FURMITY

Take some new Milk or Cream, and boil it with whole Spice. Then put in your Wheat or Pearl Barley boiled very tender in several Waters. When it hath boiled a while, thicken it with the yolks of Eggs well beaten and sweeten it with Sugar. Then serve it with fine Sugar on the brims of the Dish.

TO ROST A HAUNCH OF VENISON OR CHINE OF MUTTON

Lard it with Lard and stick it thick with Rosemary. Then rost it with a quick fire. When your meat is rosted, serve it with sauce, and strew salt about your Dish.

TO ROST A WHOLE PIG

Put such a Pudding as you love into the belly of it. Stick it with Thyme. Then spit it and lay it down to the fire. Baste it with

Butter. Set a Dish under it to catch the Gravie, into which put a little sliced Nutmeg, a little Vinegar and a little Limon and some Butter. When your Pig is rosted enough, serve it in this sauce to the Table with the Head on.

TO BAKE A TURKEY OR CAPON

Bone the Turkey, but not the Capon. Parboil them, and stick Cloves on their brests. Lard them, and season them well with Pepper and Salt. Put them in a deep Coffin [= pie-crust] with good store of Butter, and close your Pie and bake it. When it is quite cold, serve it in, and eat it with Mustard and Sugar. Garnish it with Bay Leaves.

TO MAKE A PIGEON-PIE

Take half a peck of fine Flower [= flour], and two pounds of Butter broken into little bits, one Egg, a little Salt and as much cold Cream or Milk as will make it into a Paste. Roule it thin, and lay it into your baking-pan. Then lay in it Butter. Then mix Pepper and Salt and Butter together, and fill the Bellies of your Pigeons. Then lay them in, and put in some large Mace and little thin slices of Bacon. Then cover them with Butter and close your Pie, and bake it not too much.

TO MAKE A POTATO PIE

Having your Pie ready, lay in Butter, then your Potatoes boiled very tender, then some whole Spice and Marrow, Dates, and yolks of hard Eggs, blanched Almonds, Pills [= peel] of Citron, Orange and Limon. Put in more Butter, close it and bake it. Then cut it open, and put in Wine, Sugar, the yolks of Eggs and Butter.

TO MAKE GOOD MINCED PIES

Take one Pound and half of Veal par-boiled, and as much Sewet. Shred them very fine, then put in 2 pounds of Raisins, 2 pounds Currans, 1 pound of Prunes, 6 Dates, some beaten Spice, a few Caroway seeds, a little Salt, Verjuice, Rosewater and Sugar. So fill your Pies, and let them stand one hour in the Oven. When they go to Table, strew on fine Sugar.

TO MAKE CLOUTED CREAM

Take Milk that was milked in the morning, and scald it at noon. And when it is scalding hot that you see little Pimples [= bubbles] begin to rise, take away the greatest part of the Fire. Then let it stand and harden a little while. Then take it off and let it stand to the next day, covered. Then take it off with a Skimmer.

TO MAKE A TRIFLE

Take Sweet Cream, season it with Rosewater and Sugar and a little whole Mace. Let it boil a while, then take it off and let it cool. And when it is lukewarm put it into such little Dishes or Bowls as ye mean to serve it in. Then put in a little Runnet [= rennet], and stir it together. When you serve it, strew on some French Comfits.

TO MAKE A WHIPT SILLIBUB

Take half a Pint of Rhenish Wine or White Wine, put to it a Pint of Cream, with the Whites of three Eggs. Season it with Sugar, and beat it with Birchen Rods. Take off the Froth as it Ariseth and put it in your Pot. Do so till it be all beaten to a Froth. Let it stand two or three hours till it do settle, and then it will eat finely.

TO MAKE A SACK POSSET

Take twelve Eggs beaten very well, and put to them a Pint of Sack. Stir them well that they curd not, then put to them three Pints of Cream, half a pound of fine Sugar, stirring them well together. When they are hot over a fire, put them into a Bason. and set the Bason over a boiling pot of water until the Posset be like a Custard. Then take it off, and when it is cool enough to eat, serve it with beaten Spice strewed over it very thick.

TO MAKE GINGER-BREAD

Take three stale Manchets [= fine wheaten loaves] grated and sifted. Then put to them half an Ounce of Cinamon, as much Ginger, half an Ounce of Licoras and Aniseed together. Beat all these, and searce [= sift] them, and put them in with half a pound of fine Sugar. Boil all these together with a quart of Claret, stirring them continually till it come to a stiff Paste. Then when it is almost cold, mould it on a Table with some searced [= sifted] Spice and Sugar. Then bake it in what shape you please.

TO MAKE MARCHPANE

Take two Pounds of Jordan Almonds, blanch, and beat them in a Mortar with Rosewater. Then take one Pound and half of Sugar finely searced [= sifted]. When the Almonds are beaten to a fine Paste with the Sugar, then take it out of the Mortar and mould it with searced Sugar, and let it stand one hour to cool. Then rowl it as thin as you would do for a Tart and cut it round by the Plate. Then set an edge about it and pinch it. Then set it on a bottom of Wafers, and bake it a little. Then ice it with Rosewater and Sugar and the white of an Egg beaten together, and put it into the Oven again. And when you see the Ice rise white and high, take it out. Stick it with several sorts of Comfits, then lay on Leaf-Gold with a Feather and the White of an Egg beaten.

TO MAKE A VERY RARE ALE

When your Ale is turned into a Vessel that will hold eight or nine Gallons and that hath done working ready to be stopped up, then take a Pound and half of Raisins of the Sun, stoned and cut in pieces, and two great Oranges, Meat and Rind, and sliced thin, with the Rind of one Limon and a few Cloves, one Ounce of Coriander seeds bruised. Put all these in a Bag, and hang them in the Vessel, and stop it up close. When it hath stood four days bottle it up. Fill the bottles but a little above the Neck, and put into every one a Lump of fine Sugar, and stop them close. And let it be three Weeks or a Month before you drink it.

SELECT BIBLIOGRAPHY

SOURCE DOCUMENTS

Thomas Bird, *Monumental Inscriptions in Essex 1734–1735* (unpublished MS. Essex Record Office)

C. H. Emson (ed.), *Saffron Walden Deeds*, 6 vols (typescript, Saffron Walden Town Library)

Holman MSS. (Essex Record Office)

Mayor's Book of Saffron Walden

Poor Robin Archive (Saffron Walden Town Library)

Quarter Sessions Rolls, Chelmsford, April–July, 1651

Quendon Court Book 1528–1776

Quendon Parish Registers 1687–1732

Saffron Walden Book of the Brothers of the Holy Trinity, vols I and II

Saffron Walden Court Book 1601–1659

Saffron Walden Parish Registers 1558–1749

Will of Henry Winstanley 1645
Will of Elizabeth Winstanley 1670
Winstanley Family Archives (Saffron Walden Museum)

SECONDARY WORKS

William Addison, *Essex Heyday* (London: Dent, 1949)

Vanessa Brett, *Pewter* (Oxford: Phaidon, 1981)

K. M. Briggs, *The Anatomy of Puck* (London: Routledge and Kegan Paul, 1959)

K. M. Briggs, *The Fairies in Tradition and Literature* (London: Routledge and Kegan Paul, 1967)

Martin S. Briggs, *The English Farmhouse* (London: Batsford, 1953)

A. H. Bullen (ed.), *A Christmas Garland: Carols and Poems from the Fifteenth Century to the Present Time* (London: Nimmo, 1885).

Elizabeth Burton, *The Jacobeans at Home* (London: Secker and Warburg, 1962)

William Camden, *Britannia*, trans. Richard Gough, 2nd ed. (London: Stockdale, 1806)

Mildred Campbell, *The English Yeoman: Under Elizabeth and the Early Stuarts* (New Haven: Yale University Press, 1942)

Edward Chamberlayne, *Angliae Notitia*, 19th ed. (London: Chiswell, 1700)

Mary Coate, *Social Life in Stuart England* (London: Methuen, 1924)

Charles Cotton, *The Compleat Gamester* (London: Brome, 1674)

SELECT BIBLIOGRAPHY

Charles Dickens, *A Christmas Carol* (London: Chapman and Hall, 1901)

Charles Dickens, *The Pickwick Papers* (London: Chapman and Hall, 1901)

Charles Dickens, *The Pilgrim Edition of the Letters of Charles Dickens*, ed. Madeline House, Graham Storey and Kathleen Tillotson, vols. 3 and 4 (Oxford: Clarendon Press, 1974, 1977)

John Evelyn, *The Diary of John Evelyn*, ed. E. S. de Beer (London: Oxford University Press, 1959)

G. E. Fussell and K. R. Fussell, *The English Countryman: His Life and Work A. D. 1500–1900* (London: Melrose, 1955)

Mark Girouard, *Life in the English Country House: A Social and Architectural History* (New Haven: Yale University Press, 1978)

Roger Hart, *English Life in the Seventeenth Century* (London: Wayland, 1970)

Robert Herrick, *The Poetical Works*, ed. George Saintsbury (London: Bell, 1893)

Christina Hole, *Christmas and its Customs: A Brief Study* (London: Richard Bell, 1955)

Christina Hole, *A Dictionary of British Folk Customs* (London: Hutchinson, 1976)

William Hone, *The Every-day Book* (London, 1831)

Washington Irving, *The Sketch Book of Geoffrey Crayon, Gent.* (London: John Miller, 1820)

D. B. Wyndham Lewis and C. C. Hesltine (eds), *A Christmas Book* (London: Dent, 1931)

Philip Morant, *The History and Antiquities of Essex*, 2 vols (London, 1816)

The Path-way to Knowledge (London, 1663; 2nd edn 1685)

Samuel Pepys, *The Diary of Samuel Pepys* ed. R. C. Latham and W. Matthews, 9 vols (London: Bell, 1970–76)

Niklaus Pevsner, *Essex* (Buildings of England series) (Harmondsworth: Penguin, 1954)

J. A. R. Pimlott, *The Englishman's Christmas* (Hassocks: Harvester, 1978)

Poor Robin: an Almanack after a New Fashion (London, 1664–98)

Poor Robin, *The Protestant Almanack*, 1677–1697

Poor Robin, *The Yea and Nay Almanack for the People call'd … Quakers*, 1678–80

Poor Robins Hue and Cry after Good House-Keeping (1687)

Poor Robin's Intelligence (London, 1676–91)

Poor Robin's Jests, or the Compleat Jester (London, 1667)

Poor Robins Perambulation from Saffron-Walden to London (London, 1678)

Royal Commission on Historical Monuments (England), *An Inventory of the Historical Monuments in Essex*, vol. 1, *North-West* (London: HMSO, 1916)

Nathaniel Salmon, *The History and Antiquities of Essex* (London: Cooke, 1740)

William Sandys, *Christmastide: Its History, Festivities and Carols* (London: John Russell Smith, 1852)

Beatrice Saunders, *The Age of Candlelight: The English Social Scene in the 17th Century* (London: Centaur, 1959)

Joseph Strutt, *The Sports and Pastimes of the People of England* (London, 1801)

SELECT BIBLIOGRAPHY

Alexander Smith, *The Compleat History of the Lives and Robberies of the Most Notorious Highwaymen*, 3 vols. (London, 1719)

William Winstanley, *England's Witty and Ingenious Jester: or, The Merry Citizen and Jocular Countryman's Delightful Companion* (London, 1760)

William Winstanley, *England's Worthies* (1659)

William Winstanley, *The Essex Champion: or, The Famous History of Sir Billy of Billericay and His Squire Ricardo* (London: Blare, 1690)

William Winstanley, *The Flying Serpent, or Strange News out of Essex, being a True Relation of a ... Serpent ... seen at ... Henham on the Mount, ... Saffron Walden, etc.* (London, 1669)

William Winstanley, *Histories and Observations, Domestic or Foreign* (1683)

William Winstanley, *The Muses Cabinet, Stored with Variety of Poems, both Pleasant and Profitable* (London, 1655)

William Winstanley, *The New Help to Discourse*, 3rd ed. (London: Parker, 1684)

Hannah Wolley, *The Queen-Like Closet, or, Rich Cabinet, Stored with all Manner of Rare Receipts for Preserving, Candying, and Cookery* (London, 1670)

INDEX

INDEX